The FREE
Lifetime Cash Flow
Companion Course

www.LifetimeCashFlowBook.com

Before you read any further, go to LifetimeCashFlowBook.com. You will get exclusive access to the FREE Companion Course I created for you.

You will have access to:

- Hours of video training
- Valuable content that will help you get the most out of the book
- A full list of resources and links mentioned in the book

The materials in this FREE course are organized by the sections and chapters in the book, making it very easy to follow along. I have also included tons of bonuses, including interviews and bonus videos.

I will also be adding additional materials on an ongoing basis so go ahead and visit the website below for **Instant Access**.

See you on the inside!

www.LifetimeCashFlowBook.com

Earnings And Income Disclaimer

I don't believe in "get rich" programs – only in hard work, adding value, building a real and professional career, and serving others with excellence. This book and our programs are intended to teach you how to purchase multifamily properties. The strategies outlined in this book and our programs take a lot of work and discipline just like any worthwhile endeavor or professional continuing education program.

Please don't bother reading this book or enrolling in our programs if you believe in the "money for nothing get rich quick" myth or ideology; I only want serious people dedicated to real professional development. **As stipulated by law, KL Promotions LLC, Lifetime Cash Flow Academy LLC nor Rod Khleif can not and do not make any guarantees about your ability to get results or earn any money with our ideas, information, tools or strategies.** We don't know you and, besides, your results in life are up to you. Agreed? We just want to help by giving great content, direction, and strategies.

You should know that all products and services by our company are for educational and informational purposes only. **Nothing in this book or on any of our websites, or any of our content or curriculum is a promise or guarantee of results or future earnings, and we do not offer any legal, medical, tax or other professional advice. Any financial numbers referenced here, or on any of our sites or trainings are illustrative of concepts only and should not be considered average earnings, exact earnings, or promises for actual or future performance.** Making decisions based on any information presented in this book or in our products, events, services, or web site, should be done only with the knowledge that you could experience risk or losses just like any entrepreneurial endeavor.

Use caution and always consult your accountant, lawyer or professional advisor before acting on this or any information related to a lifestyle change or your business or finances. You alone are responsible and accountable for your decisions, actions and results in life, and by your registration here you agree not to attempt to hold us liable for your decisions, actions or results, at any time, under any circumstance.

"Through significant experience, Rod has turned his journey into an all-encompassing road map with this book. This is not a 'quick fix;' he arms you with lessons and tools that will help you achieve incredible long-term wealth, but that will also help develop you on a personal level. These lessons are invaluable and Rod has laid them out in a way that anyone can understand, whether you're in the business or not."

Ken McElroy, Rich Dad Advisor to Robert Kiyoski and Bestselling Author

"Buy this book! Read it, apply it, and prosper! Rod has vast experience in the real estate world, both in up and down markets. Rod is a strategic thinker who knows how to reduce risk and increase gains in both types of markets. It's rare to find someone who brings this kind of experience to real estate and is willing to share their knowledge."

Diane Kennedy, Rich Dad Advisor to Robert Kiyosaki and Bestselling Author

"I really appreciate the detail Rod put into his book, How to Create Lifetime Cashflow Through Multifamily Properties. The section regarding adding value to your property was of particular interest to me as a long time multifamily owner. The discussion of expense reductions was a great reminder that a dollar saved might be a little more important than a dollar earned. This is a solid book and will benefit any investor who aspires to own multi-family rentals."

Al Williamson, www.LeadingLandlord.com

"An entertaining and practical read guaranteed to help new and experienced real estate investors make more money today and leave a legacy for generations to come."

Julie Broad, Author of More Than Cashflow

"How to Create Lifetime Cashflow Through Multifamily Properties is a great resource for aspiring multifamily investors to begin their education in the exciting field of multifamily real estate investing."

Douglas Bibby, President of the National Multifamily Housing Council

Want To Have Rod's Team Work With You To Create Your Own 90-Day Multifamily Action Plan?

If you have the desire to build Lifetime Cashflow for yourself and your family by joining a group of motivated, supportive, and successful apartment investors with over 45,000 units.

Scan the code using your smartphone camera to book your call with Rod's team to apply:

or go to https://calendly.com/rk-success-agents/lcfbook

Join hundreds of students in every corner of the United States and Canada, Mexico and Europe.

The Warrior Community is our group of motivated and engaged real estate investors, who are each taking massive action to build a portfolio of multifamily properties for legacy cash flow by implementing Rod's strategies for personal and financial success.

Think you might be a fit? Scan the code below using your smartphone camera to book a call with Rod's team to apply!

Go visit www.MultiFamilyCommunity.com right now and join this incredible free peer group!

You are invited to join the Multifamily Community Facebook Group

Here is what you will find inside the private group:

- Peer-to-Peer mentoring;
- Networking with potential partners and investors;
- A passionate group of people all interested in multifamily investing;
- Industry experts AND...
- My team and I answering questions to accelerate your learning curve.

Fans and readers of *"How to Create Lifetime community CashFlow Through Multifamily Properties"* make up an incredible community of motivated action takers that want more our of life. As the writer of the Lifetime CashFlow book, it was my responsibility to create an online space where aspiring multifamily real estate investors could go to connect, share ideas, ask questions, get encouragement, peer mentor, find accountability partners, and learn and grow in this exciting business.

Just go to MultiFamilyCommunity.com to join the "Multifamily Real Estate Investing Community" on Facebook with over 40,000 members. Here you'll be able to connect with an incredible peer group of investors who are already taking action on their dreams of building *lifetime cash flow* with *multifamily properties.*

You will be blown away by the caliber of the members in this community. Go there to give, but expect to also get incredible value from this incredible group of investors.

I check up on the group regularly and moderate the community. I look forward to seeing you there!

Let's Connect!

If you'd like to connect with me personally on social media, follow:

Facebook: https://www.facebook.com/RodKhleifofficial

LinkedIn: https://www.linkedin.com/in/RodKhleif

Instagram: https://www.instagram.com/Rod_Khleif

Twitter: https://twitter.com/RodKhleif

Please feel free to send me a direct message on any social channel. I love getting them and I respond to each one.

You can ask me a question, or leave a comment.

Talk soon!

Contents

Dedication

This book is dedicated to my mother, Zwaantje Jacobs. Burdened with the difficulty of raising five boys with very little money or resources, she inspired me immeasurably. From her courage and hard work, I learned my work ethic and love of real estate.

Thank you, Mom.

Foreward

As a real estate "artist," who has gone from flipping $50,000 houses to creating then selling the most expensive spec home in the world at $50 million, I know good real estate advice when I read or hear it. I also know bad real estate advice, and believe me there's plenty of it. I've been at this for 30 years and most real estate books aren't worth the paper they're printed on.

Rod Khleif's new book *How to Create Lifetime Cashflow Through Multifamily Properties* is radically different. I encouraged Rod to change the subtitle to "How to Create GENERATIONAL CashFlow Through Multifamily Properties." That's how important and impactful Rod's book can be, but only if you methodically and patiently apply Rod's wisdom. Rod possesses a PHD in real estate, if there were such a thing, so now it's time to go to school!

How to Create Lifetime Cashflow Through Multifamily Properties will open your eyes to the incredible opportunities in multifamily real estate, massively expand your knowledge on the subject, and provide you with the aspiration to take action towards becoming a successful multifamily investor. For anyone considering multifamily investing, I know of no better book on the subject than the one you're holding right now.

This book was written to be an essential textbook for the new multifamily investor, an instruction manual. I suggest you study this book many times over and learn from Rod's years of experience and expertise in multifamily investing.

Rod has also included important content related to the psychology of your success. It's well known that 80% of your success is related to your psychology and only 20% is related to the actual mechanics. Throughout this book you will be motivated, encouraged, and inspired to take action towards reaching your goals both as a successful multifamily investor and in your personal life.

With four decades of experience in real estate investing, Rod has earned a reputation as one of America's top real estate professionals and top multifamily investing coaches. Among Rod's many talents, he has the unique ability to simplify the complex which makes him an outstanding teacher and coach.

For the last three decades, Rod and I have traveled similar paths as real estate professionals and dedicated philanthro-capitalists. We know and deeply respect each other's work. We both incorporate sharing our blessings with those less fortunate as a major driver in our lives. Through my foundation; The Caring House Project, I have provided housing and a self-sustaining existence for 10,616+ people in Haiti. Through Rod's foundation; The Tiny Hands Foundation, he has provided over 65,000 children and families in need with food, Christmas toys, backpacks, and school supplies.

I trust that you will enjoy and benefit from reading this book, just as I did. In it you will learn the path to creating *lifetime cash flow through multifamily real estate investing*, and if you're really good, maybe even generational cash flow!

Frank McKinney (www.frank-mckinney.com), Real Estate Artist,
Philanthro-Capitalist and 5x Bestselling Author, including "Burst This!
Frank McKinney's Bubble-Proof Real Estate Strategies."

Introduction

Have you ever struggled financially? Have you ever wanted more? As you were growing up, did you have everything given to you or did you have to fight and work hard for everything you wanted? I'd like to take a few minutes to tell you a bit of my story. I have had fantastic successes and some equally spectacular failures, which I call my "Seminars."

I was born in The Hague, Holland in 1960. I lived in Holland until the age of three, and then I moved to Israel for three years. I immigrated to the United States with my mother and my brother when I was six years old. We made the journey in a large ship, and I remember my mother crying when she saw the Statue of Liberty in the New York Harbor. That was in 1966.

We quickly ended up in Denver, Colorado, where I lived for the next 30 years. We didn't have many possessions or very much money. I was forced to wear clothes from Goodwill because we couldn't afford to buy new ones. My brothers ended up wearing my Goodwill hand-me-downs. We couldn't afford to buy real milk, so we had to use the powdered kind. My mother bought bread from the day-old store because it was half price.

We had love, but not much else. I am eternally grateful, however, that my mother showed me the value of hard work. She had a side babysitting business in our home. She taught us that if we wanted anything, we had to work for it.

My First Date With Real Estate

My love of real estate started when I was 17. Three years prior, my mom used her babysitting income to purchase the house across the street for $34,000. When I was 17, she told me it was worth $55,000. Even though I flunked basic math in high school, I could do that calculation. When I realized that she made $21,000 in three years, I decided that I was going to get into real estate.

I went to real estate school when I was 17. I had my broker's license by 18. I was ready to make the big bucks. The only thing was, I had absolutely *no clue* what I should be doing. I rented a bench at a bus stop at the end of my street and put my name and picture on it. I never got any business off of it, but my mom was very proud.

Eventually, things got better and I sold my first house. My first year in real estate I made $10,000. My second year in real estate I made $15,000.

Then I went to work for a broker who was also a brilliant salesman. He gave me confidence in my sales abilities, and by my third year in real estate, I made over $120,000. It was my learning the business and developing my confidence and self-esteem; and that made all the difference.

This is when I started buying houses for myself to rent out. I found out a long time ago that if I was willing to do what other people weren't, I could make a lot of money. I literally went out every night for years and talked to people that were in foreclosure. I would either list their properties for sale or buy them. I ultimately bought 500 houses in Denver, which I'll talk about later. I then bought 200 houses in Memphis, and ultimately bought more than 1,300 homes in Florida.

To date, I have owned over 2,000 houses and multiple apartment buildings. I did a lot of successful flips, but I quickly realized that was a job. I then bought real estate to hold onto for the long term. I knew that if I wanted long term cash flow, I would need to hold onto my real estate.

I now realize that I love helping other people learn how to do real estate. I get immense pleasure from seeing other people succeed in this business. And I hope I can help you on your journey as well.

I Discovered Visualization

Although I did not realize what I was doing at the time, I learned to set goals and use visualization to manifest what I wanted in life at an early age.

Throughout my twenties, I listed a lot of property for sale. I bought and sold houses, and I lived fast and loose. I cut a lot of unncessary corners and took a lot of unnecessary risks. When I look back on that time, I feel lucky I survived. I made every mistake in the book and more, but I was smart enough to learn from those mistakes.

During those learning experiences, I discovered some of the primary things that impacted my life over the long-term. Unfortunately, I was successful with single-family homes. I say "unfortunately" because had I not been successful with single family homes, I probably would have focused on multifamily and not suffered the huge setbacks that I'll tell you about next.

My First Big Seminar

I experienced my first real estate market crash in Colorado during the late 80s. Things got really tough. I remember having to sell my cars to make payroll payments to my staff. I also ended up losing my home to foreclosure.

This was a very low point in my life. At this point, I had zero money. I was painting houses for a few hundred dollars just so I could eat. Finally, one day while I was painting this house, I literally had a meltdown and started crying. I eventually threw the paint brush down and pulled myself up by my bootstraps. I swore I would never feel sorry for myself like that again.

Everyone in the Denver real estate market at that time got their butts kicked. People were so afraid of real estate that nobody was buying anything. HUD and VA had a lot of foreclosed properties they were trying to sell and were offering investors financing for only $500 down! So, I jumped back into the real estate market. When it was all said and done, I ended up accumulating over 500 houses and numerous apartments in Denver.

Now when you become successful, it is easy to get a big head and think that you can replicate that success in any environment. I made the huge mistake of asking my cousin, who lived in Memphis, Tennessee, to send me a HUD foreclosure list. I saw three bedroom properties listed for $8,000, $5,000, $3,500, and as low as $1,500. I immediately jumped on a plane to Memphis, and in a little over a year, I had purchased 200 houses there.

This turned out to be one of my "Seminars." Memphis is a tough market to manage remotely particularly with single family homes.

The House On The Beach

To finance my dream house on the beach and to help finance purchasing rentals in Florida, I sold all of my real estate in Denver in the late 90s, which was a big mistake. Had I held onto those properties, they would all be paid off by now. Their combined worth would be over $150 million dollars, and they would be cash flowing around $500,000 a month. This is why I no longer believe in selling real estate. I am a real estate "buyer," not a "seller."

From there, I started purchasing homes like crazy in Florida. I have, to date, owned over 1,300 homes and apartments in Florida. I thought that I had a fantastic business model. Then 2008 happened, and I was again proven wrong.

My Life-Changing Mentor

In 2000, I completed construction on my beautiful luxury home on the beach. What was interesting is even though I had accomplished a 20-year dream, I was quite depressed. One evening, I was floating in my incredible pool, looking up at this incredible huge mansion on the water, yet I felt crappy and depressed.

One of the things I learned in that moment was you should never get close to the attainment of a goal without having other goals lined up. I needed a vision for the future. Like the good book says, "Where there is no vision, the people perish." I started reading motivational books to build myself back up. I bought books from Zig Zigler, Dale Carnegie and, luckily, I came across this book from the greatest mentor I've ever found in my life: Anthony Robbins.

The book was titled "Unleash the Power Within." I was so impacted by it, I attended one of Tony's seminars a few months later. I was simply blown away by his technology and strategies as a result I have attended at least three or four of his seminars every year for the last 16 years.

One of the many gifts I learned from Tony was the desire to always work on myself – to work on my relationships, emotions, business strategies, time management, and my health. I have tried to greatly improve my life in every one of those areas.

Regretfully, when I did get real with myself, I realized that I was in the wrong relationship. We have two beautiful children, who are the loves of my life, and telling them we were getting a divorce was the absolute worst day of my life – even to this day. I also lost my beautiful home on the beach in the divorce.

But, it's important to know what I learned. I've learned that whenever you have something negative happen in your life, there is *always* a silver lining. It may not show up for years, but it is there. My new home on the water is significantly more beautiful than what I had before, and I am now married to the absolute love of my life. The thing to remember is, when you encounter stebacks like this in life, there will always be a silver lining.

My Second And Largest Seminar

As I was building my portfolio of Florida homes, I quickly learned that low-to-middle-end Florida single-family homes are almost impossible to cash flow because of the high costs of turnover, taxes, and insurance. My multifamily properties cash flowed well, but not my single family houses.

I did not really pay much attention to the fact that I occasionally had to sell or refinance houses to have enough cash to operate. I was convinced that Florida was recession-proof. I had the mentality that 80 million baby boomers were getting old and would keep the market in Florida going forever. **I was wrong.**

I was only focused on the value of my real estate instead of the cash flow. In 2006, the value of my real estate appreciated $17,000,000 in just one year! I thought I was untouchable. My head swelled so big that I could barely get it through the door. I had done the math on that $17 million and how it broke down over that year. It worked out that I was earning over $326,000 per week or over $8,000 per hour based on a 40-hour work week. **I was insufferable.**

When people get like this, God will usually teach them a lesson. And that is exactly what happened to me. When the market crashed in 2008, I couldn't sell those homes. Nobody could. I couldn't even refinance them. It was a real problem.

Prior to the real estate crash of 2008, all of my properties only had a 30% loan-to-value. For every dollar of property value, I only owed 30 cents of it. Even with that great loan to value ratio, when the market crashed, it crashed so hard that I was underwater. I couldn't hold on. One of the hardest decisions I ever had to make was to stop making payments on hundreds of my houses.

This crash turned out to be my largest "Seminar" ever. It was a $50 million dollar "Seminar." I chose to write this book because of that "Seminar" and the lessons I learned from it!

The Most Important Lesson I Learned

The most important real estate lesson I got from this crash was that my apartment complexes were cash flowing just fine through all of the turmoil and loss of value. Had I just been in multifamily assets, I would have done fine. That is why I started my podcast, "Lifetime CashFlow Through Real Estate Investing" and it is why I wrote this book. What is important to remember, is that real estate goes in cycles. There will definitely be another contraction at some point in the future. When that happens, I don't want anyone to experience the same "Seminar" that I did.

I wrote this book to be more like a textbook. I want it to be a road map for you to learn this business. I hope you can grow and learn from my experiences, my triumphs and my mistakes.

Just in case you missed it, I also created a FREE companion course that includes tons of additional content. Before you go on to Chapter 1, visit the website below for instant access. I promise you... it will provide you with tremendous value.

<u>www.LifetimeCashFlowBook.com</u>

Chapter 1
Goal Setting

It has been said that "Where there is no vision, the people perish" (Proverbs 29:18). There is a lot of truth in that statement. Every successful person that I have met, or read about regularly, sets goals.

Success does not just fall into a person's lap. Success does not mean that a person is wiser, has more resources or is more educated. Success comes from the journey you experience when you set measurable goals. Entrepreneurs, real estate investors, professional athletes, you name it, the most successful people in any field regularly set goals.

> *Where there is no vision, the people perish.*
> Proverbs 29:18

Your brain has a reticular activating system (RAS), which is a portal that filters nearly everything that comes into your mind. It separates all the thousands of bits of information that your brain has to process. The RAS decides what you pay attention to and what floats out of your head.

For example, have you ever purchased a new car and realized you never really noticed that car before you bought it? Now that you own one, you see them everywhere. That is the RAS at work!

Your RAS is a great goal setting tool. If you regularly write out your goals, the reticular activating system will log them into your subconscious. You will be surprised how quickly this can help you accomplish your goals. Your brain is very powerful. The simple act of writing things down you want triggers your RAS to start looking for the things that will help you achieve those goals!

Don't be one of those people that goes through life blindly letting life push them in one direction or another. Take control of your destiny by regularly writing down your goals and *why* you must achieve every one of them.

Course Corrections

Achieving your goals is never a straight line. If you know your outcome, when you do get off course, you can refocus on that outcome and change direction as needed.

An airplane in mid-flight is typically off course around 90% of the time, but it always ends up landing in the right spot. How does that happen? The pilot keeps making small course corrections. Those continuous little corrections keep them on their planned path (or shall we say heading towards their goals).

I know if you're reading this book, you have likely written goals somewhere. But the sad reality is that *very few* people have actually taken the time to *write down their goals* and why they want them. That is one of the major reasons many people have unrealized dreams.

Realize your dreams by writing down your goals.

There really is no excuse for not writing down your goals. Sit down and do it. Stop reading for a minute and do it right now. Your future self will be glad that you did.

If you go to work on your goals, then your goals will go to work on you. Life is not about the destination. It is about who you become in pursuit of your goals.

It has also been said, "Ask and it will be given. Search and you will find. Knock and the door will be opened for you." (Matthew 7:7) If you never ask, if you never get up and search, if you never get brave and knock, then how can you expect to get?

- You cannot change your destination overnight, but you can certainly change your direction over night.
- Build your own dreams or someone else will hire you to build theirs.
- People overestimate what they can do in a year and grossly underestimate what they can accomplish in a decade.
- If you can dream it, you can achieve it.

Believe me. I am living proof that you can control your destination through goals!

Chapter 2
Finding Your "Why"

Now that you have your goals written down, let's talk about the importance of your *"why"* when it comes to setting your goals.

Some people only think about goals around the new year. By January 15th, they have forgotten all their goals and have fallen back into the same old habits, pressures, and rat races. Others create goals as often as once a month, once a week, or even daily. The problem is, even though these people may have written down their goals, very few will write down *why* these goals are a must. They have a goal, but they have not defined the motivation that will drive them to meet their goal.

What they do not realize, is that it is the why –the reason you want to accomplish those particular goals – is the most important component of goal setting. Setting a goal without clearly defining why that goal is a must, is simply a waste of time. It is the *why* that drives you! It is the *why* that will get you up out of bed to go kick butt in your business and your life. It is the *why* that will keep you going into the night to achieve everything you want.

It is the WHY that drives you! With that being said, do you know *why* you want to achieve your goals? Do you know *why* you want to be a financial success? Do you know *why* you want to be a great parent? Do you know *why* you want to get in great shape? If you don't, then you need to take the time to review each of your goals and list your whys.

Did you notice that I said, *"your whys?"* The motivating force behind why you have set one goal, will not necessarily be the same reasons why others have set that same goal. If you want to be truly motivated to accomplish your goals, then you need to figure out why *you* want to meet *that* goal.

Anytime I write down a goal, I put down both the positive and the negative compelling reasons why that goal is a must. Let me give you an example of what I am talking about. Let's say, that my goal is to create $100,000 a month of net positive cash flow from my multifamily real estate investments. It is important to use words in your whys that evoke emotion. Words are very powerful.

Examples of positive whys could be:

- So I can help other people and live my mission!
- So I can live the incredible life I've always dreamed!
- So I can buy my amazing wife everything she wants!
- So we can build the house of our dreams!

Examples of negative whys could be, for example:

- So I don't think to myself, "Why didn't you pull out all the stops?"
- So I don't live with regret.
- So I don't have to live paycheck to paycheck.
- So my spouse and my kids don't think that I could have done more.

I know the negative reasons may sound harsh, but the leverage from your negative whys will motivate you just as much as the positive reasons. By stacking both the positive and negative emotions, it makes these goals or outcomes even more compelling.

It is the emotions buried in your whys that will drive you to action.

Just know this: You are going to get knocked down. You are going to get beat up and bloodied during your journey towards your goals. The reasons, the motivations, and the whys have to be strong enough to make you get back up and not give up. Your why has to be strong enough and powerful enough so you do not get knocked out.

There is a big difference between getting knocked down and being knocked out. A solid why will give you the strength to take your licks and get back in the game. You can become a prize fighter when you are motivated to win – no matter how many times you drop.

It is the emotions buried in your whys that will drive you to action.

There is this great saying from Eric Thomas, "When you want to succeed as much as you want to breathe, that is when you will be successful." This is why you should never just write your goals without writing why you want to reach those goals.

Chapter 3
The Power Of Visualization

I want to take the opportunity to speak to you now about visualizing and manifesting what you want in life. I have used visualization for decades. It has only been within the last eight years or so that I actually realized what I was doing. I want to talk to you about this for a few minutes.

"The mind is everything. What you think you will become."

~ **Buddha**

"Whether you believe you can do a thing or not, you are right."

~ **Henry Ford**

"Dreaming is not enough. You have to go a step further and use your imagination to visualize, with in- tent! Forget everything you've ever been taught, and believe it will happen, just as you imagined it. That is the secret. That is the mystery of life."

~ **Christine Anderson**

Visualization is an incredibly powerful tool for manifesting what you want in life. Professional and Olympic athletes are taught to visualize their entire race or event before they start. They have even hooked athletes up to sensors and had them visualize the race. The sensors showed that the muscle groups were firing off in the same sequence as if they were actually racing.

Guang Yue, who is an exercise psychologist from the Cleveland Clinic Foundation in Ohio, studied visualization of workouts versus those who worked out without completing the mental exercise in advance. His study found a 30% muscle increase in the group that visualized the workout before performing it.

Mental practice can change the outcome of the game. Take Natan Sharansky, for example. He played mental chess while spending nine years in a Siberian prison with half of the time being spent in solitary confinement. When interviewed later on why he continued to mentally play chess, he is quoted as saying, "I might as well use the opportunity to become the World Champion!" Well, that visualization paid off. In 1996, he beat World Champion chess player Garry Kasparov.

According to Jim Carrey, when he was 19 years old – long before he was famous – he wrote himself a check for $10 million "for acting services rendered" and dated the check Thanksgiving Day, 1995. He carried that check around in his wallet. Eventually that check got worn and tattered because he kept using it as his visual motivational aid.

Right before Thanksgiving Day in 1995, he found out his movie *Dumb and Dumber* was going to earn him his $10 million dollars. Now that is an example of visualization.

Have you ever sat and dreamed about having an incredible car or nicer house? I did a lot when I was growing up. I can tell you my own stories about the power of visualization. They relate to obtaining the cars and houses that I wanted. Now, I will say that these types of things don't motivate me like they previously did, but they certainly did at one time.

I remember when I started out in real estate, I drove a four-door Ford Granada. I remembered always wanting a Corvette, so I clipped a magazine picture of a Corvette from a magazine, and taped it to the visor in my Granada. I looked at it just about every time I got in the car. Within a year or two, I had that Corvette.

Then there was the time that I remember wanting to own a Ferrari 308 GTS just like Tom Selleck drove in the TV show *Magnum P.I.* I put a picture of that Ferrari on the visor of my Corvette. Within a couple of years, I bought a Maserati Merak which looked almost identical to the Ferrari that I wanted.

Ever since I was a teenager, I have always wanted a Lamborghini. While I was growing up, I had posters in my bedroom of Lamborghinis with sexy girls. Then my seven year old son caught the fever. He had posters of them in his bedroom. He even had models of various Lamborghinis. The crazy thing is that he actually had a model of the exact Lamborghini that I ended up buying about a year later, down to the exact same color.

He told me that he actually visualized me bringing him to school in it. He told me how exciting that would be for him. So here we were both visualizing the same future event.

As I already mentioned, for years I used to visualize having a house on the beach. I visualized the palm trees. I pictured my wife and me walking on the beach. I could see the beautiful home that I would own. After all that powerful "daydreaming," in 2000, I built a 10,000 square foot home on the beach in Sarasota. I'm not sharing this with you to brag. I am sharing my personal story and experiences with visualization and manifesting, along with those I have researched, to help you understand the power of visualization.

Visualization works! You might be thinking right now, "Oh, that's just goofy" or maybe you think that you are just too practical or rational to consider something like that. But, my friend, if that is how you feel, I want to warn you that you are making a big mistake.

I am a very visual person by nature. I like to have pictures of the things that I want to manifest in my life. If you go in my office or my exercise room, you are going to see pictures of the material things that I am trying to manifest in my life now. Having a representation of my goals helps me visualize having them.

I have read many books on visualization and attracting what you want into your life. they all have one common theme: **they suggest visualizing what it is you want and seeing it as if you already have it.** That visualization needs intense emotion and *Visualization needs intense* genuine gratitude. I have *emotion and genuine gratitude.* applied what I learned, and it has worked for me. It doesn't matter whether you want to call it visualization, meditation, daydreaming, or even prayer. If it helps you get what you want in life – then just do it!

"Thoughts are things."

~ Napoleon Hill

If you change your thoughts, you can change your world.

Chapter 4
Cash Flow Is King

The old rules of real estate were seemingly set in stone. They had nearly become gospel. We have been repeatedly told that if we want to make money in real estate, then we needed to follow the rules and focus on "value."

The rule of the real estate game was to buy low and sell high. Gains in real estate were tied to appreciation. If you bought a home for $150,000 and held it for five years with an annual average appreciation rate of 4.57%, you could expect to sell that home for $187,550 and secure a capital gain of $37,550. The cash flow was hardly considered. The focus was all on appreciation.

Investors were nearly 100% focused on the resale value. Most of the emphasis was placed on flipping the property. Wholesalers and flippers multiplied like rabbits and the name of the game was quick cash.

We Need To Play By Some New Rules

The new rules of real estate are simple the focus is now on cash flow. If you are interested in buying real estate of any kind, you need to leave the old rules behind and focus on cash flow, not value. Even if you are buying and holding only single family homes, creating a stable and sustainable net positive cash flow should be your most important parameter.

I have over 39 years of real estate experience. I have lived through huge increases in net worth and cash flow. I have also been affected by huge downturns and loss of value. As I mentioned earlier, during the 2006 calendar year, I saw a $17 million increase in the value of my real estate holdings. I subsequently lost that immense gain and a lot more in the 2008 real estate crash.

Had I focused on cash flow rather than the net worth of my assets, I would have survived that downturn without an economic loss. When 2008 hit me, I saw my single family homes get devastated financially but my multifamily properties cash flowed just fine.

What did this difficult life event teach me? Real estate values are irrelevant. Cash flow is king! If you want to weather any future economic storms, then cash flow is the key to survival. Creating a reliable, dependable, and self-sustaining source of income is the fuel that builds investment momentum and creates sustainable real estate generated wealth. This is exactly what I have learned from my own personal experience, as I explained in the Introduction. *It all boils down to creating cash flow.*

Many skilled and extremely experienced real estate investors that I know, and others that I have interviewed, believe that the real estate market will likely experience a significant pullback in the near future. They do not expect it to be as large or as devastating as the 2008 Great Recession, but it will be significant. If your real estate investments are based on current market value and future appreciation, and not cash flow, then you will suffer when this happens. If, however, you focus on creating sustainable cash flow, then no matter what the real estate market does in the future, you will be prepared to come out on top.

An investment property that has a meager cash flow is simply a "hope for the best" and a "wait and see" property. This creates a huge risk for the investor. What if the market does not produce the increased income or value growth that you hoped for? What if after years of counting and depending on market value appreciation, it dissolves before *Real estate values are irrelevant. Cash flow is king!* your eyes? Millions of investors and homeowners saw that happen in 2008. All they were left with was a barely adequate income stream that left little, if any, room for further capital investment.

Worse yet, they lost their entire investment. However, if your initial investment criteria is based on locating strong cash flow opportunities, then future value appreciation is only the icing on the cake.

A Shift In Investment Strategies

With a growing desire to create an ultrastable real estate investment strategy, I have completely shifted my course of investment. Because of my less than optimal history with single family properties, I now focus almost entirely on multifamily properties that offer an opportunity to create value or that build on existing value. When I speak of increasing value, I am referring to improving the net operating income of the properties I purchase.

Market appreciation is an inherently risky method of creating sustainable increases in property value. On the other hand, there is a direct correlation between the net operating income and a multifamily property's market value. If an investor can increase the net operating income, there will be a measurable increase in property value. I will explain the details of examining and measuring net operating income, and the incredible value of improving it, in much greater detail in Chapter 16.

What Does It Take To Be Successful In Real Estate?

You need to understand that regardless of what the so-called real estate "gurus" tell you, whether you heard it at a weekend seminar or read it in one of their popular books, there is no getting rich quickly in real estate.

The systems that they pitch are much like one of those rapid weight loss pills you see advertised. You spend substantial money upfront for a miracle process. You take the pill, and for the first few weeks it looks like it is going to work. Then the results diminish. Nine times out of ten, you end up right back where you started and usually more miserable than when you started.

If you go off with one of these "gurus," you will end up paying thousands of dollars to get your hands on a "new" money making system. They are all going to tell you basically the same thing. "Flipping or wholesaling properties is the way to make quick cash in real estate." They promise that you can generate thousands or even tens of thousands of dollars off of every transaction and that soon you will be rolling in money.

You cannot just make a few phone calls, create a website, and sign a few purchase agreements to rake in the money. Successful people know it takes focus, training, and hard work to become successful and wealthy in anything – and that includes real estate.

That being said, you can become very wealthy from acquiring and owning income-producing investment properties and ultimately not have to work, if you don't want to. However, it will take education, patience, and perseverance. It is going to require locating properties that can support dependable, sustainable, and steady cash flow.

There are also huge opportunities to be found in the duplex, triplex, and small to mid-sized apartment building markets in this country. These properties fly under the radar of the big players, but they can make you very wealthy. I will show you how to locate great deals, negotiate for them, write offers, fund them, reposition them and then manage them to create significant and reliable sources of lifetime cash flow.

There is a continuous need for affordable housing in the United States. According to the U.S. Department of Housing and Urban Development, "An estimated 12 million renter and homeowner households now pay more than 50% of their annual incomes for housing.

A family with one full-time worker earning the minimum wage cannot afford the local fair-market rent for a two-bedroom apartment anywhere in the United States." The need continues to grow, and it does not look like it will be solved in our lifetime.

There is also an incredible opportunity to acquire mobile home parks in this country that have less than one hundred spaces. Large investors and REITs rarely look at these smaller-sized parks. I have friends and family that are making a fortune buying and repositioning mobile home parks right now.

This low hanging fruit is rarely picked by the large sophisticated real estate players. Of course, you can compete against these high-roller investors, if you want to make your money via larger-scale investments. Many of my friends compete with them. With the smaller properties; however, you will be regularly dealing with less experienced sellers that lack the skills of large-scale investors. You will also be dealing with much less competition.

Having a portfolio of positive cash-flowing properties will enable you to not only weather the storm but to profit from it as well.

The rules in real estate have changed. Rather than focusing on property appreciation and the resale value, it makes more sense to put the primary importance on developing stable sources of recurring monthly income. Regardless of the direction that the real estate market takes, having a portfolio of positive cash-flowing properties will enable you to not only weather the storm, but to profit from it as well.

Chapter 5
Understanding Real Estate

What else can you buy that someone else pays for? Income producing real estate is the only investment that offers this benefit. A good real estate investment will ensure the debt that you carry on your property is paid for by the rent received from your tenants. They will pay for all of your expenses, including your maintenance costs, property taxes and property insurance. They will also give you incredible tax benefits. Most importantly, your tenants will provide you with consistent monthly lifetime cash flow.

True Wealth Is Cash Flow

About 30 years ago, I met an old, real estate investor in Denver, Colorado. He owned numerous free and clear apartment buildings in the city. He told me something that I have never, ever forgotten. He said the smartest thing I could ever do would be to buy

True wealth is a consistent, unassailable stream of monthly income.

multifamily real estate and let other people pay it off. Then I would end up like him, with numerous income properties that were paid off and producing lumps of cash every month. That old man said, if I really wanted to make "buckets and buckets of money," there was no better way to do it than by buying multifamily properties. That conversation has stayed with me for more than 30 years.

"Can't you make a lot of money from appreciation?" some may ask. Absolutely. You can make a ton of money from appreciation, but as we discussed earlier, you can also lose just as much money if you only focus on appreciation.

We are living in volatile times. We are part of a global market. We cannot afford to think that just as long as the economy in our market area is strong, then real estate values will increase. International and political events can affect our economy in ways that are hard to predict. New lending policies can be implemented that dramatically affect the real estate market. Demographics and population mobility can impact

You will not lose if you pay attention to net cash flow.

21

your market. All of these factors are outside of our control. They all can impact market values and overall price appreciation. Real estate always goes through cycles. You have to be able to survive the down cycles that I described.

You will not lose, however, if you pay attention to net cash flow. If all you get from this book is that simple message, it will completely change your real estate career.

Buying Property With Other People's Money

Have you ever wished that you could buy lots of real estate with none of your own money? Have you ever found yourself thinking, "I know I would love buying real estate, but I don't have any money right now?" I know I did at one time.

It is going to take confidence. You can develop that confidence by gaining enough knowledge of this industry. This will give you the ability to influence people to invest with you. I bought 500 houses and apartments with partners in Denver without spending a cent of my own money. You can do this also. Study this business through books and courses and go look at deals. At some point, you will have enough knowledge of this business and the confidence to influence investors to invest in your deals.

Leverage The Power Of Leverage

Investing in real estate offers another incredible advantage over other investments: it is the power of leverage. It is possible to own and control incredible amounts of real estate *utilizing leverage.*

Broadly speaking, leverage refers to the ability to use other people's money to buy real estate. When a buyer obtains a mortgage in order to purchase a particular piece of real estate, he or she is using leverage.

The buyer will pay a down payment, say 20%, of the purchase price and then finance the rest. He or she is using other people's money to invest in real estate. Utilizing investors and lenders in this way will greatly improves an investor's cash-on-cash return.

What is cash-on-cash return?

You will hear this term over and over again. It is important to understand what it means and how it affects your return on investment. Cash-on-cash (CoC) return refers to the return an investor receives on the actual out of pocket money he used to purchase the real estate.

I will give you two simple examples to illustrate the power of leverage and its impact on CoC returns. One example will not use any leverage, and the other example will utilize it.

Example One: Let's say you purchase a duplex for $100,000. You pay cash for the property. After your first year, you pocketed $10,000 in net operating income before taxes. If you divide the $10,000 of net operating income into your out-of-pocket purchase money of $100,000, you will have a 10% CoC return. We could say that was a good investment, right?

What would happen if you leveraged the property using other people's money by obtaining financing?

Example Two: Using the same property, you decide instead to put down 10% of the purchase price, or $10,000. The seller carries the remaining $90,000 on an interest only loan at 4%. You will still earn $10,000 of net operating income. You will also need to make interest payments on the loan for an annual amount of $3,600. This means that you would net $6,400. If you divide $6,400 into your out-of-pocket investment of only $10,000, you now have a 64% cash-on-cash return on that exact same piece of investment real estate.

Who wouldn't want to earn an annual return of 64% on their money? *That is the power of leverage.*

Tax Benefits Add Value To Real Estate

If you are looking for a way to lower your income taxes, then there is no better vehicle for tax benefits than owning real estate. I'm sure you've heard that many of the super wealthy pay little or no taxes. Why? Because they own lots of real estate and they maximize all of the allowable real estate deductions.

These tax benefits add incredible value to real estate acquisitions and ownership. Being able to deduct things like mortgage interest, repairs, property insurance, depreciation and other expenses can improve the return on your investment.

Even small-time investors can reap large tax benefits by owning real estate. You're able to write off travel expenses to view the property and can often even recoup more by deducting your home office. In fact, the first few years of deductions can be greatly enhanced by optimizing cost segregation for a property's depreciation.

Simply put, cost segregating the depreciation is the process of breaking down each depreciable component in the property like windows, doors, appliances, heating and cooling systems, and depreciating them individually based on their individual useful life. You will need to work closely with your CPA to make sure it is done correctly, but it can save you, and your investors, thousands in taxes over the first few years of ownership.

The Key To Earning Is Learning

If you want to be successful in anything, including real estate investing, you need to immerse yourself in it completely and be constantly learning. Once, when I had a portfolio of about 800 houses in Florida, my young son came to me and asked why I was still going to so many real estate seminars, and why I had so many books in my library about real estate investing. I told him that the key to earning is continual learning.

Learning real estate is not about attending one seminar and being done. Making a living off real estate investing requires continual growth and education. The key to earning is *learning* and *learning* and *learning*. You need to study it, wallow in it, and most importantly, you need to learn to love it. I love real estate investing because I love real estate and everything about it. I love learning and expanding my knowledge base. Real estate investing isn't work, it's fun. I love playing with real estate. So, if you are getting started in real estate, be sure to associate pleasure with learning this incredible business.

Four 'Must Do's' To Speed Up Your Success

Investing in apartments can seem intimidating. Here are four areas of focus that will help demystify the process and help you become an expert as quickly as possible with the fewest mistakes.

1. Study Real Estate

Do not "dabble" in apartment investing. We have seen dabblers get crushed. Being successful at anything, including becoming wealthy with apartments, requires commitment. You have to invest your time and energy to be a huge success. Like I mentioned before, success in real estate is directly linked to education and learning.

You can listen to podcasts about real estate investment. You can take our free companion course that will help you assimilate this book, available at www.LifetimeCashFlowBook.com.

You can also take advantage of coaching programs such as our comprehensive course and coaching program, or one of our three-day live bootcamps events. You can sign up for these programs and learn more at www.RodKhleif.com.

Regardless of whether you join our program or not, it is critical that you are constantly furthering your education about apartment investing.

2. Start Kicking The Tires On Deals

In addition to learning through books, courses, and podcasts is to start looking at properties. You need to get out there and kick the tires. Develop relationships with apartment brokers in the market(s) you are interested in and have them start sending you deals.

Even if you don't buy any of these deals, this is a critical component in your education. Look at these properties, evaluate rents and expenses, and start to develop an intuition about apartment investing and its nuances. This is just as important as the book study. Ignore either of these training methods and you are going to make mistakes. How do I know this? Regretfully, I got that "Seminar" out of personal experience.

3. Pick The Markets To Focus On

While learning the business, we suggest you study in your own backyard. After you develop some confidence and experience, narrow your focus into a maximum of four different markets so as not to get overwhelmed. It is critical to only invest in markets you have studied, know, or have resources in. The four places we suggest are:

- Your backyard

- Another place you know very well (where you grew up or went to school)

- A place with boots on the ground (friends/family live there)

- A place you want to retire

Narrowing down your focus to those four markets will keep you focused and keep you busy! Building a solid network in those markets will ensure you're ready to take on a property in a place you enjoy, know well and have interest in.

Decide On Your Ideal Size And Style Of Property

Multifamily, like other sectors in real estate, has numerous types and sizes of properties. There are A, B, C, and D areas as well as A, B, C, and D class properties. We personally like to focus on B and C properties in A and B areas. Later, in this book, I will further qualify what determines the type of area and property classification.

Naturally, the size of multifamily properties can go from a duplex all the way up to a 500+ unit apartment complex. You will need to determine your investment criteria, such as the size and type of property and your market areas, before you reach out to brokers. This will not only help you gain credibility with the brokers, but it will also minimize feeling overwhelmed and help you stay focused.

Build A Killer Team

Have you ever thought, "How can I do this by myself?" I know that when I started, I felt that way. There are so many things to learn and so many pieces to understand.

The good news is no successful person in this business does it alone. Every effective real estate investor has to put together a team of experts. Your team will have your back. They will help you make good decisions and help protect your financial interests.

Commercial Real Estate Brokers

Choose brokers that work full-time in the area you want to purchase your investment properties in. Developing relationships with brokers in your tarket markets is critical to your success. Broker relationships can make you wealthy.

Real Estate Attorney

Get the best real estate attorney that you can find in your area. Make sure that they specialize in commercial real estate. Ideally, find an attorney that actually owns multifamily real estate. They will be worth every cent you spend.

Commercial Lenders, Brokers and Bankers

Remember how we discussed the benefits of leverage? Creating working relationships with commercial lenders and local bankers is one of the best ways to use leverage to your benefit. We prefer local and regional banks over large national banks for small apartment buys. They are much easier to work with.

There are also excellent commercial real estate lending brokers you will utilize when you get into the larger deals. It never hurts to start developing those relationships right from the start.

Accountant

Real estate is all about money. You are going to need a great accountant to help you keep as much of it as you can. Look for one that does a lot of work for real estate investors. They will need to understand how to utilize cost segregation so you can maximize all of your tax deductions.

Bookkeeper

Speaking of money, hiring someone to do your bookkeeping will help you keep all your rents and bills straight. It will also reduce the time and costs associated with your accountant. There are some great virtual bookkeeping companies out there. Very few people enjoy doing bookkeeping, so outsource it. This will allow you to focus on finding great deals.

Property Management Company

I encourage you to manage your income properties yourself; but I also encourage you to have an experienced property manager on your team. It will help you to build credibility with lenders and brokers, especially if you are new to real estate investing.

Insurance Agent Broker

All of your investment properties are going to need to be insured. Not all insurance policies are alike, nor will all policies give you sufficient coverage. Choosing an experienced and highly recommended insurance agent can save you thousands and ensure that your investments are completely protected.

The best way I know to find the different members you need to make up your team is to ask for referrals from some of the other people on this list. Ask the broker who are the best bankers or attorneys. Ask the attorney who they think is the best real estate CPA and then ask for an introduction.

To download a MS Word team-building checklist visit:

www.LifetimeCashFlowBook.com.

Chapter 6
Business Structures

While owning your personal homestead in your own name is customary, most real estate investors seek the benefits of other business structures to purchase, hold, manage, and sell their investment and income properties.

When we talk of "business structures," we are speaking in particular about legally registered companies or corporations. The most common types of business structures include:

- Sole Proprietorship
- S-Corporations
- C-Corporations
- Living Trusts
- Limited Liability Partnerships (LLP)
- Limited Partnerships (LP)
- Limited Liability Companies (LLC)

Some of these business structures are much better to hold real estate investments than others. It is important to understand how these entities can protect your investments, impact tax liability, and affect future ownership transfers. More complete protection can be created by layering several business structures on top of each other, which creates an effective veil blocking access to you and your personal assets.

The Benefits Of Business Structure

We live in an age of lawsuits. Lawsuits are filed for the smallest infractions, inconveniences, and injuries. It is not uncommon for the judgment to far exceed the losses.

To help protect real estate investors from lawsuits that could strip the owner of their personal assets, investment real estate should be held in some sort of business structure other than the owner's personal name.

This serves as a protection for your personal assets. A judgment would be limited to the assets held within that business structure (in most cases). Assets you own outside of that business structure - including your personal home, automobiles, bank accounts, investments, and assets held in other businesses you own or control - would be safe from the judgment.

There are also tax benefits in forming business structures to hold investment real estate. It should be noted, however, that different business structures are taxed differently and have different tax benefits. Before setting up a particular ownership medium, make sure you are fully informed on how that business structure will affect your bookkeeping, payroll and tax filings.

Have you ever worried about what might happen if you get sued once you own some valuable properties? This was something that really troubled me. Over 35 years ago, I started using entities to protect myself when I started acquiring a lot of properties. I had heard horror stories of people losing everything through frivolous lawsuits. I knew I did not want to lose everything I had worked so hard to acquire over *Maximize the legal and tax benefits by forming the correct business structure.* something that was not even in my control. Back then, LLCs were not being utilized. The entity of choice for holding real estate was limited partnerships. I formed lots of them for peace of mind. You'll learn below that LLCs are now the vehicle of choice, but I want to educate you first about your other options.

Types Of Business Structures Available

Most new investors are concerned about liability protection and how to structure their real estate purchases, as I was. There are many different ways to use different business structures to own, manage, and bequeath real estate. Before we discuss how to balance multiple business structures to create the ultimate real estate portfolio protection, we need to first understand the basics.

Sole Proprietorship O ers Self-Employment Taxes & No Liability Protection

Purchasing an investment property as a sole proprietor is the easiest business structure, but in my opinion, a foolish one. To purchase real estate under a sole proprietor business structure, you simply use your legal name and social security number. The difficulty with owning investment or income-producing real estate as an individual is the lack of protection from lawsuits.

If a tenant sues you and receives a judgment against you, all of your personal assets can be used to pay for the judgment. This would even include your homestead.

Another disadvantage of owning investment real estate as a sole proprietorship is that all non-passive income is subject to the 15.3% self-employment tax. *Do NOT own investment real estate in this manner.*

Corporations O er Protection But Double Taxation

Corporate real estate ownership creates a barrier between the owner's outside assets and the assets owned by the corporation. A judgment in a lawsuit will be limited to the assets owned by the corporation, not any outside assets owned by members of the corporation.

There are two types of corporations from a taxable standpoint: C Corporations and S Corporations.

C-Corporations (C-Corps)

C-Corps are stand-alone entities that pay taxes on the income they generate. There is a downside to the C-Corp when it comes to real estate ownership. It is the reason why most property investors do not use C-Corps. Income earned in a C-Corp is subject to double taxation. Income is first taxed under the corporate entity and then taxed on an individual level when that income is distributed to shareholders. Any rental income that is not dispersed regularly to the shareholders is subject to a 15% Personal Holding Company (PHC) tax.

Another C-Corp tax hardship is that rental losses cannot be passed on to shareholders. Losses stay within the C-Corp and can be applied to future years. This may not seem bad until you sell the property. If the property were held for more than a year, the gain (equity) would be taxed at the corporate tax rate of up to 23.8%. Any distributions would be taxed again at the personal income tax rates applicable to each shareholder receiving a distribution from the sale.

S-Corporations (S-Corps)

S-Corps, on the other hand, are not subject to double taxation like a standard C-Corp. The profits and losses pass through to the shareholders. The major benefit for an S-Corp is that the shareholders can also be employees that receive a salary. Any profits above and beyond the "employee's" reasonable salary can be paid as bonuses or distributive shares. Distributive shares are not subject to Social Security and Medicare taxes.

Additionally, some expense deductions can actually be deducted twice—once for the income taxes and once for the payroll taxes. For example, self-employed health insurance, health savings account (HSA) contributions, and SEP-IRA contributions are deducted from the net operating income and are not subject to Social Security or Medicare taxes.

However, there are some S-Corp limitations for real estate investors:

a) Some states don't recognize the IRS S-Corp v. C-Corp distinction and treat all corporations like C-Corps;

b) Non-US persons and certain entities cannot participate as shareholders (other C-Corps, Partnerships, etc.);

c) Only one class of stock is allowed so all shareholders must be treated equally;

d) No more than 25% of the income of an S-Corp may be passive income (including rental income). Excess passive income is taxed at the highest applicable rate.

Before setting up a S-Corp, consult with your tax advisor to ensure this legal structure will benefit your business plan and real estate portfolio.

———

A corporation (C-Corp or S-Corp) can establish credit and borrow funds in the corporation's name. This can be a huge asset in creating funding to purchase real estate investment properties. Additionally, stockholders of a corporation are not personally liable for the debts and obligations of the corporation. Their personal liability is limited to their actual monetary investment.

A big benefit with S-Corps is that they are not subject to corporate tax. Net income flows through the S-Corp into the personal tax return through Form K-1, subject to the limitations described above.

A major problem with holding real estate investments within either type of corporation is the high capital gains tax rate. The regular capital gains tax rate can be as high as 35%. A 1031 Exchange can be used to defer payment of the capital gains, but all shareholders must be included in the 1031.

In general, corporations are not good entities for holding real estate investments over the long-term. The double taxation of a C-Corp combined with high capital gains taxes makes this unappealing, to say the least. The 25% limitation on passive (rental) earnings may make the S-Corp a less than ideal choice.

Partnerships O er Tax Advantages With Limited Liability

Partnerships are not subject to double taxation . In fact, they are not a taxable entity at all. All net operating income or losses are passed through to the individual partners. Income taxation is processed on a personal or partner level. There are two types of partnerships applicable to real estate investors, "General Partnerships" and "Limited Partnerships."

While single taxation is preferable, General Partnerships do not benefit from the liability shield created through corporate ownership. In the event of a lawsuit, the personal assets of the general partners could be subject to the judgment. In a General Partnership, each general partner is personally liable for all debts and obligations of the partnership.

One way to limit liability within a partnership is to create a Limited Partnership (LP), comprised of one or more general partners and limited partners. This business structure provides a measure of liability protection to the limited partners (passive investors), but not the general partner, who remains liable for all acts of the Limited Partnership. A limited partner cannot materially participate in the business without losing its limited liability.

Passive income generated from rental properties can be passed through to the partners, who pay taxes on their individual earnings from the Limited Partnership. Partnerships were very big when I first started in real estate, but they are used less now because of the advantages of utilizing a Limited Liability Company or LLC.

Limited-Liability Companies O er A Liability Shield Plus Tax Benefits

All of this complication in real estate ownership has led lawyers and accountants to find a business structure that is perfectly designed for real estate ownership; one that would feature the tax benefits of a partnership but the liability protection of a corporation. A Limited Liability Company (LLC) is that hybrid solution.

What makes an LLC the best choice for most real estate investors? Broadly speaking, an LLC provides all of its owners the same liability protection found under corporate ownership while benefiting from single level taxation similar to partnerships. LLCs are easy to form and are recognized as a real estate business structure in all 50 states.

It should be noted, however, that many lenders will not write a mortgage for an LLC unless there is sufficient assets and equity within the LLC to secure the debt service. That is unless you are obtaining a non-recourse loan, which we will describe further in this book. If the loan is full recourse, it is common for lenders to require a personal guarantee from some or all of the members.

LLCs are much simpler to manage than S and C Corporations. Upon the formation of the LLC, an operating agreement is created. It specifies, like a corporation, how and by whom the company will be managed, each member's (owners') name, the amount of ownership interest held by each member, and other items, such as voting rights, transferability of interests, and withdrawal or removal of members.

Unlike a corporation, however, LLCs do not require an annual meeting or formation of a board of directors. The management of LLCs is much more flexible than corporations. An LLC may be managed directly by its members (all of whom actively participate in its operation) or by a designated manager who may or may not be a member.

Under an LLC, someone can be paid a salary, which may be deducted from the profits before the net operating income is passed through to the members.

Another benefit of an LLC is that certain profits, losses and tax benefits can be allocated any way you like among members. It does not need to be based on the percentage of ownership. This is very helpful when approaching investors for your deals. Some investors need more tax deductions than others, so you can negotiate to give them what they need, with more cash flow to other investors.

Misconceptions About LLCs

There are several misconceptions about LLC, including the misconception that LLCs provide complete and utter protection of the personal assets of the property owner. This is not entirely true.

LLCs provide a shield against a member's personal assets if the lawsuit comes from within the LLC. For example, if a tenant sues the landlord because they slipped and fell on ice, the judgment will affect the LLC that owns the property, not you as a member or manager, or your personal assets, such as your home.

On the other hand, if you are driving to repair a unit and you hit a pedestrian on the way, you are not only personally liable for the injury but, because you were "working" for the LLC, it could be named in the lawsuit, as well.

Additionally, if you are a negligent property owner, your LLC may not guarantee protection. If you know that the steps leading up to the apartment building are dangerous and you do not fix them, you may personally be held liable for the damages if someone is injured. The same can be said if you break the law, such as committing fraud, misrepresentation or other illegal acts.

Your personal assets can also be at risk if you personally guarantee a loan on real estate owned by your LLC. This is a common practice required by lenders when there is a full recourse loan and a limited amount of equity within the LLC. In the event that the LLC defaults on the loan, you will need to use your personal assets to cover the debt.

It is also important to separate the LLC from your personal finances. You cannot use personal finances to cover expenses within the LLC. The LLC needs to be a separate legal entity with its own bank account. If the veil is too thin, an attorney can show that it is a company in name only (alter ego) and attempt to "break the corporate veil" to come after your personal assets.

To summarize, an armslength LLC will legally protect investors from contractual liability. Combine your LLC protection with a hefty umbrella liability insurance policy to ensure the greatest degree of legal protection.

How To Use Business Structures

Initially, you will want to keep your business structure simple and straightforward. This could simply mean placing your investments in a LLC. As your portfolio grows, a more structured business plan should be developed.

Keep Each Property Separate

In addition to an umbrella liability insurance policy, it is wise to keep income properties in separate LLCs. In the event of a lawsuit on one property, the others are protected.

Consider you own two apartment buildings. One building has 6 units and is valued at $230,000 and the other has 25 units with a market value of $750,000. Both are held in the same LLC. The portfolio has a net worth of $980,000.

One icy morning, one of your elderly tenants in the six unit apartment building steps outside to pick up the paper. She slips on the ice and breaks her hip. She receives hip replacement surgery and spends the next eight months in a nursing home. Her family files a lawsuit in the amount of $550,000. For the sake of this argument, let's say that the liability insurance only covered half of the judgment; there would be a remaining liability of $275,000, which is greater than the value of the building where the tenant slipped.

Since both properties are held by the same LLC that was sued, the 25 unit apartment building must also shoulder the cost of the judgment. If they were held in separate LLCs, the second building would not have been affected.

When each property is placed in separate LLCs, it is called a "silo" investment. Hypothetically, if one silo situated in its own field burns down, all the other silos are intact. The financial loss is minimized. If a lender forecloses on an investment property held in a single purpose LLC, all the other holding companies or LLCs owned by the investor are disconnected from that foreclosure.

In order for this arrangement to work to your benefit, each LLC needs to be a stand-alone business with separate books and records. If they share the same bank account, it may be argued that they are all part of the same entity.

Keep Your Portfolio In A Holding Company

It is a smart move to separate the business side of real estate from the ownership side. It is wise to have each investment property in its own LLC, *except* in states with steep LLC costs, especially when investing in single family properties.

Typically, you would create a holding company that owns all your interests in the individual property LLCs. This holding company does *not do* anything. It only *owns* the investments.

There are some additional costs involved in creating this LLC and a little more time to handle the accounting side. That being said, there are quite a few benefits to placing each income producing property into a separate business structure.

The most obvious benefit is that it creates another layer of separation between you and your personal assets and investment properties. In a big ugly lawsuit, it will be much more difficult to pierce such a thick veil of ownership.

Holding companies are an easy way to transfer ownership across multiple properties. Assume that John Doe owns a portfolio of 100 income properties throughout Cleveland. He decides to bequeath partial ownership to his relatives before he passes. Filing deed changes on over 100 different properties and dividing up the ownership among the relatives can get complicated fast.

Instead, John Doe owns a single LLC that acts as a holding company and owns all the real estate within it. Rather than deed a percentage of the ownership rights on each individual property, he simply transfers membership interests in the holding LLC to his heirs.

Create A Management Company

Let's say you have taken my advice, and you have each of your investment properties filed away in individual LLCs. All of the interests in the LLCs are owned by an umbrella holding company. If you have decided to self-manage your income properties, like I suggest, then it is a good idea to create a separate management company to handle the day-to-day operations of your properties.

In this case, an additional LLC or even an S-Corp is beneficial. As an employee of this management company, you can be paid a salary. This entity may earn fees or even a share of distributions from the LLCs it manages. If done correctly, this structure may eliminate self-employment taxes and increase write-off expenses for the management company, which effectively lowers your personal income.

Before setting up a management company, consult your CPA or tax advisor to discuss which legal entity creates the best tax shelter for you. Make sure you are only managing properties you have ownership interest in. Otherwise, your company may need a licensed real estate broker as one of the owners.

Create A Construction Company For Fix Up & Flips

If you will be rehabbing your investment properties before you resell or lease them, consider creating an additional company to function as the general contractor. Before doing this, you may need to research licensing requirements related to acting as a general contractor in your state. Also, you should consider getting appropriate general contractor's liability insurance for this entity.

Since this company would not be receiving passive rental income, but rather function as a service business earning active (versus passive) income, you should consider the benefits of creating an S-Corp rather than an LLC. Though an LLC is more than adequate and is much better than a simple Sole Proprietorship, in some cases an S-Corp may offer a greater tax shelter when it comes to non-passive income.

Chapter 7
Types Of Apartments

Types Of Multi-Family Properties

Multifamily housing spans both the residential and commercial categories. Income properties of four units or less remain on the residential side. Apartment buildings of five units or more units are classified as a commercial investment.

Have you ever been intimidated by the thought of buying larger properties? I was intimidated. That's why I started with duplexes, then four units, eight units, 22 units until I graduated into larger properties. That's how I started to build a comfort level. There are successful people that start with larger properties and if you understand this business well, you can do that. That said, don't be afraid to start small and build your confidence as you buy larger and larger assets.

Residential Two-to-Four Family Properties

Income properties with four or less rental units are classified as residential real estate. This can be advantageous when getting a mortgage. Residential classification creates competitive lending terms, low down payment requirements, low interest rates and long-term, fully-amortized financing. The downside is that Fannie Mae properties have a ten -property mortgage cap.

Multifamily rental properties that are classified as a residential investment include the following:

- Duplex (2 Units)
- Triplex (3 Units)
- Quadraplex (4 Units)

Duplex properties can include a main residence with a guest house, mother-in-law apartment or separate living unit. Triplexes or (three-family) properties are comprised of three units per parcel. Quadraplex or (four-family) can be small apartment buildings or townhouse-like units built back-to-back or side-by-side.

The secondary mortgage market (namely Fannie Mae and Freddie Mac) limits the number of residential mortgages that any one real estate investor can hold at a time. The maximum number of allowable simultaneously financed properties, including the primary residence, is 10.

Fannie Mae has a 5-10 Properties Financed program, but many banks don't participate in it. This is because the underwriting required for a fifth home is much more intensive. Most lenders place their personal limit at four properties.

5 – 10 Property Finance Criteria

- 25% down payment for properties with one unit
- 30% down payment for properties with two to four units
- 30% equity required for all refinances
- 720 minimum credit score
- No mortgage late within the past 12 months on any mortgage
- No bankruptcies or foreclosures in the past seven years
- Two years of tax returns showing rental income from all properties
- Six months of PITI reserves on each of the financed properties

How to Get Around the Finance Limit

- Finance some properties in your name and the others in your spouse's name. Each owner will need to independently qualify for each mortgage.
- Purchase investment properties with seller financing.
- Finance properties using bank "in-house" loans that are not sold to the secondary mortgage market.
- Purchase builidings with more than five units to qualify for commercial funding.

Apartment Buildings

Multifamily properties containing five or more units are considered commercial investment. Any debt service is also classified as a commercial mortgage. These are the property classifications of multifamily investments:

- Garden Complexes: 3 Floors or Less
- Walk-Up: 4 to 6 Floors, no elevator
- Mid-Rise Projects: 4 to 8 Floors with elevator
- High-Rise Projects: 9 Floors or more with elevator
- Special-Purpose Housing: Targets a particular population group such as:
  - Student Housing
  - Senior Housing
  - Subsidized Housing

Apartment Building Classification

Within each property type, there are four levels of property classification. This breaks down each investment into a category that describes not only the construction style, but also the general condition and construction quality of the investment.

Class A MultiFamily Properties

This is the premier level of property classification. It is the most expensive per unit category. Class A properties include the following markers:

- Usually constructed within the past 10 to 15 years
- Properties constructed more than 10 years ago have been substantially renovated, updated, and modernized.
- High Functionality
- High quality construction with highest quality materials
- Modern construction methods
- Energy efficient construction standards
- High quality landscaping, attractive rental office, and high end amenities
- Very good location in newer growth areas
- Often located in the luxury market
- Central Business District properties often include retail and/or offices on the first few floors and are usually of high rise construction.
- High rental rates
- Low vacancy
- High appreciation

Class B MultiFamily Properties

This property class typically serves middle-income tenants. This classification can vary greatly depending on the construction standard, economic age, and functional utility of each individual property. The general classification is as follows:

- Generally built within the previous 15 to 30 years
- Very good to good functionality
- Minor, if any, deferred maintenance
- Very good quality construction with upgraded materials
- Utilizes modern construction methods
- Good quality landscaping and mid-range amenity package
- Good location in older, stable areas
- Very good rental rates
- Lower vacancy
- Very good appreciation

Class C MultiFamily Properties

This class of apartment building is where properties in average condition commanding mid-to-low rental rates fall. This property class has the highest potential for growth and increase of property value, that is, if they are properly acquired and skillfully managed. Look for the following characteristics within this class:

- Generally built within the last 30 to 50 years
- Average to reduced functionality
- Generally composed of outdated design styles and is in need
- of renovation and modernization.
- Suffers from some deferred maintenance
- Dated exterior
- Limited amenities, if any
- Average location in older, declining or stable areas

- Good to average rental rates
- Average vacancy
- Average appreciation
- Average to good cash flow

Class D MultiFamily Properties

When you hear the term "slum-lord," these are the types of properties they own. In addition to the poor overall conditions, these properties are also affected by locational obsolescence. They are often found in the roughest of neighborhoods and have low market appeal. Rents charged in this area are low and tenant defaults are high. This is the cheapest category of multifamily housing, and are often purchased for the income stream rather than any future appreciation value. Typically these investment types have a high rent-to-purchase price ratio but also suffer from above average vacancy. You can identify a Class D property by the following features:

- Built within the previous 30 to 100 years
- Usually functionally obsolete
- Marginal and outmoded construction methods and with average to inferior products
- Typically poorly maintained
- Short remaining economic life
- Dated exterior in fair to poor condition
- No amenities
- High risk locations in older, declining or potentially declining areas
- Management intensive
- High turnover
- Very little, if any,appreciation
- Can be very good cashflow

I owned a lot of Class D properties when I first got started in Denver. I had properties that briefly became crack houses. People were killed in and around these properties. I was constantly evicting bad tenants and fighting to keep decent tenants. I made good cash flow, but it was a lot of work and stress. Personally, I wish I had focused on better properties from the start. If I had, I would have had time to acquire more properties.

Unfortunately, I was too busy managing tough properties to focus on buying *more*. I don't want to discourage you from this investment class, but I believe there are easier ways to make big money.

Classifications And Their E ect On Financing

Investors aren't the only ones who must weigh the risk versus value when it comes to an income-producing multifamily property. Lenders will also carefully examine the property classification and the future probability of a return on that investment. This is why higher classed properties are marketed for a *much* higher purchase price. Not only is the condition superior and the quality of tenants higher, but the potential for long-term investment stability is stronger. Consider how the mortgage market reacts to each property classification:

Class A Assets

- More financing options
- Lower interest rates
- Longer fixed terms and amortization schedules
- Up to 80% LTV
- Asset is the primary source of collateral
- Non-recourse loans available

Class B and C+ Assets

- Fewer financing options
- Average to good interest rates
- Fixed rate loans with an average 5-10 year balloon
- 75-80% LTV
- Non-recourse loans available

Class C and D Assets

- More Limited financing options
- Higher interest rates
- Floating interest rates
- 65-75% LTV
- Personal guarantees regularly required

Classifications And Their Typical Purchasers

Competition can be intense within the multifamily market. Sole proprietor investors can find themselves competing against partnerships, companies, pensions, REITs and corporate investors. Knowing who you will be coming up against, and why they are seeking a particular property classification, can help you to enter a transaction more prepared.

Class A Assets

- Primary purchasers include institutional investors such as life insurance companies, pensions, REITs, large and very sophisticated, experienced investors
- CAP Rates average 4% to 6%

Class B Assets

- Primary purchasers include institutional investors, REITs, corporations, private investment groups and high net worth individual investors
- CAP Rates average 6% to 8%

Class C Assets

- Primary purchasers include private investment groups and individual investors
- CAP Rates average 7% to 10%

Class D Assets

- Primary purchases are individual investors
- CAP Rates start at 8% and often exceed 10-12%

Understanding Property Classifications

Choosing properties in a classification which matches your investment goals is critical. Apartment buildings within these different classifications will produce entirely different investment results.

Class A Investments

Investors look to Class A properties for their portfolio stability. The capitalization rate is low, yet the stability is high making it a low-risk investment.

- Higher purchase price per unit
- Lower cashflow
- High appreciation potential
- Extremely stable investments

These properties are primarily purchased for their value appreciation.

Class B Investments

This category of apartments provides for a balance of portfolio stability and cash flow. The capitalization rate is higher than Class A investments indicating a slightly greater investment risk.

- Moderate purchase price per unit
- Average to good cash flow
- Good appreciation potential
- Stable investment

These properties are purchased primarily for value appreciation but stable cash flow is also a consideration.

Class C Investments

Properties in the Class C segment create the basis for steady increases in cash flow. Capitalization rates are attractive and reflect the balance between cash flow and investment risk.

- Moderate to average purchase price per unit
- Good cash flow
- Average appreciation potential
- Average investment stability, which is dependent upon sound management strategies.

Class D Investments

Investors that purchase Class D properties are not looking for value appreciation. They are concentrating solely on cash flow. These are considered high risk properties, which is reflected in their very attractive CAP rates.

- Low purchase price per unit
- Can be very good cash flow
- No appreciation potential, depreciation probable
- High risk investments
- Above average capitalization rates

Before purchasing an apartment building, each investor must define their individual investment goals, their experience, long-term portfolio direction, target cash flow and investment resources. These factors will help an investor to purchase properties in a class that will help them meet their investment goals.

While Class D properties can be very attractive due to their low purchase price and high cash flow, the day-to-day management is very time-intensive. High capitalization rates are often contingent upon minimizing maintenance costs. Investors rarely realize value appreciation when it comes time to sell. Financing can also be a challenge.

Non-institutional investors often turn their focus to Class B and C properties. Under sound management, these properties have the potential to create positive value appreciation. The capitalization rates are comparative to other investments. The cash flow is also attractive.

Chapter 8
Taking Action On a Deal

Finding great deals is a lot like looking for treasure. It's my favorite part of real estate investing. It reminds me of a time, years ago, when I was in the basement of one of my houses in northeast Denver. I was instructing my maintenance man on what I wanted done to finish the basement. I reached up and put my hand on one of the ceiling beams and a gold coin fell on the floor. I thought we had struck treasure. We tore that basement apart inch-by-inch but that one coin was all we found. Finding properties is like looking for those gold coins.

Maybe you've heard the old adage, "You make your money when you buy." This is the absolute truth. When you find a great deal, you need to be ready to move on it – whatever it takes. When I was still buying single-family homes, I learned a really important lesson that I want to share.

I had just moved to Florida from Denver, and I was rapidly acquiring single-family homes and small apartment buildings. I discovered this area in Port Charlotte, Florida that had waterfront homes and lots on direct access canals to Charlotte Harbor. You could literally take a sailboat from your backyard out to the harbor and into the Gulf of Mexico. There were no bridges blocking your access.

I found five of these canal homes priced under $130,000. I also found three or four lots on these canals for under $60,000. Investors that lived and bought in that area did not realize the incredible opportunity in these properties. They were desensitized to the opportunity because it's easy to become numb to what you see every day. I bought all five houses and the four lots as quickly as I could. Those five houses went up in value from $600,000 to $850,000 in just a few short years.

If you find a deal, do whatever it takes to make it happen.

This scenario could very well happen to you, if you act on an opportunity. In your search for great multifamily properties, you may also need to go outside of your market area. It is not entirely uncommon for investors in a particular market to not see opportunities right in front of their noses. They have been desensitized to what is right in front of them. You could bring a fresh perspective in that market area that makes these value-add opportunities more obvious to you.

Remember, if you find a deal, do whatever it takes to make it happen. I have even put properties on my credit cards because the deal was so fantastic; I did not want to miss the opportunity.

In order for you to be ready to jump on a perfect deal, you need to educate yourself and be on the lookout. You need to be ready. You need to do careful due diligence. And most of all, you cannot be afraid to take action.

How To Be Ready To Act

For every investor that purchases an income-producing property, there are probably 1,000 wannabe investors that are too afraid to act. They suffer from "analysis paralysis." They spend too much time learning how to find the perfect deal. They study over and over and take no action to buy. They have this impossible list of qualifiers, but they lack motivation to act. They never advance past the learning stage.

If you want to make a success of real estate investment, you must set yourself and your investment plan into motion. You must situate yourself so that when you locate the income property that meets your criteria, you are ready to pounce on it. There are three steps to get prepared:

1. Know how to identify a good investment deal.

2. Create a conduit that leads to successful funding.

3. Create a team to help you close the deal.

How To Identify A Good Investment Deal

Up to this point, much of what we have discussed has been basic information to help you choose an investment property to meet your personal criteria.

We have encouraged you to focus on cash flow, not resale value. If a property cannot create *Falling in love with a property is a* a positive cash flow *mistake you cannot afford to make.* from the start, you do not have a viable investment opportunity.

When you work with a team, they will help you identify money-making investment opportunities. They will help you take the emotion out of the purchase. Falling in love with a property is a mistake you cannot afford to make. You must make sure that each and every deal meets the financial qualifiers for

48

profitability from your due diligence of the market and that property.

Your investment criteria should be clearly set down in writing. You will want to establish a written list of specifications that a potential investment opportunity must meet. Your clearly defined investment criteria will help you learn your market. It will help you compare different investment opportunities objectively and compare them apples-to-apples.

It will also speed up the property qualification process, allowing you to analyze more properties quickly. It will also give you credibility with brokers and investors. Your property investment criteria list may include items such as:

- What is the property type and classification?
- What type of area is it?
- How many units does it have?
- How many vacancies does it currently have?
- What is the current rent versus market rent for each unit?
- What is the asking price per square foot?

To obtain a free copy of our investment criteria checklist, visit

www.LifetimeCashFlowBook.com.

Create A Conduit That Leads To Successful Funding

Before you can move on a great deal, you must figure out how you are going to pay for the purchase. This is the part in the process that brings many investors to a halt. They can identify a good deal, but they have not arranged a means to pay for it. Before they can get funding, the deal is gone. Do not let that happen to you.

No matter whether you are planning on getting conventional financing or hard money loans or are working towards owner - carried financing, you are going to need a down payment.

You will need a minimum of 25% of the purchase price to put down, but you should plan on 30%. You are also going to need to have funds to cover your due diligence, closing costs, capital expenditures, and some interim operating capital funds. Larger investments will also be required to have capital reserves set aside, as well.

This can be a challenge to pull together. This is where advanced planning is necessary. As I will mention later in this book, you should be working on putting together funds while you are looking at deals. This money can come from savings, friends, family, or investors. And, of course, you need to put a killer team together like I described previously.

Chapter 9
What Markets Focus On

Irrespective of the story in the previous chapter, if you are a new investor, I highly recommend focusing on your own market, or your "backyard" first. There could be diamonds in your backyard. While you can find deals in most markets, focusing on your backyard will accelerate your learning curve.

In referencing your backyard, we are talking not only about a specific town or suburb, but also an area where you could realistically self-manage the properties. Would you be willing to take a day to travel to the property to perform some work and then travel back? If so, then that could reasonably be your "backyard." In some cases, that could be your entire state, but as I suggested earlier, start out close to home.

Why Backyards Are Better

There are a lot of reasons why buying in your backyard is much better than going outside of your market area. First and foremost, you will have much more personal experience in that market. Firsthand knowledge of the interdependency within a market, its trends, its hot areas, and its war zones will make an investing decision much easier. It is going to be much simpler to identify a good buy when you already know the market. It is also going to be much harder for you to get taken advantage of.

Second, properties owned in your backyard will be simpler to manage. Third, buying in your market area is going to make it much easier to assemble your team of professionals. You have friends, family, business associates and others that you can ask for referrals. I get the best referrals for team members from local real estate brokers and attorneys.

Fourth, you will build more respect and credibility. Out-of-town landlords can sometimes be taken advantage of. You are unknown in that market area. How can a tenant, repairman or other real estate professional trust someone they do not know?

Some banks will not loan to out-of-state investors or borrowers they do not have existing relationships with. On the other hand, if you own properties in the market area where you are well known, your respect and credibility grows. If your properties are well-managed, it will be easier to get local funding. Professionals, in and out of the real estate field, will respect and trust you.

You Must Know Your Market

Now that I have hopefully convinced you to stay nearby when studying this business, at least initially, I want to discuss some of the factors to consider when you are selecting your target market(s).

We are going to take the remainder of this chapter and really drill down into the facts and data that you must sift through in order to get to know your market areas from an investor's point of view. Before you start looking around for an investment property, perform your due diligence on the market.

Growth

When you buy an investment property, you are investing into a future income stream. This means that you will want to try to predict whether there will be income growth, or at least stability, in the future. You cannot just depend on the condition and quality of the property. The market area must also be considered. Ask yourself the following questions:

- What is the current population of this sub-market or neighborhood?
- What is the historic population over the past 5 to10 years?
- Is the population growing?
- Is there job growth?
- What are the income demographics for the area?
- Is the per capita income increasing?

You can get this information from **www.BestPlaces.net** as well as other sites listed in the "Where to Find the Data" chapter below. When you have all this raw data, you need to know what to di with it. The conclusions that you draw from this data will help you to predict the risk involved in a purchase within this sub-market area.

- What do you believe is causing the growth? What is drawing people to move into this area? It could be job creation, medical facilities, education, retirement or recreation. Knowing who is moving in can help you to choose properties that cater to this category of renter.

- How does the per capita income compare to the area's cost of living? This can give you an idea of whether the income is trying to catch up to the cost of living or whether there is room for rental rate growth. Look for areas where the rent to income percentage is below 30% to maximize the potential for rent increases.

Employment

When you are investing in apartments in a particular market, a good understanding of the current employment situation is important. Employment brings jobs, jobs bring population and that increase creates demands for housing and commercial support services.

- Is there job growth?
- Are new businesses and industries moving into the area?
- Where are they moving?
- Are businesses moving out of the area?
- What is the major employer(s) in the area?
- What is the unemployment rate?
- How does the present unemployment rate compare to historical figures?
- Is the unemployment rate going up or down?

Take these figures and see how they interact. Consider the following factors:

- Is there one major employer or many? You do not want to invest in a one-horse town. When that horse dies, the town dies and your income dies with it. It is way too risky. This could include areas near some military bases. Look for areas that have a variety of major sources of employment.
- How does the unemployment rate compare to national averages? What does this tell you?
- Where is the area of commercial growth? Is there housing in and around that area? New commercial construction can open the door for some very lucrative multifamily housing opportunities. Tenants like to be close to shopping, schools, medical services, and work.

Development

Area development – both residential and commercial – is a good indicator of whether you are buying in an expansionary market or a deflating one. Do not just chase current development. Talk to the local economic development office to find out where the future development is moving. Ask them these questions:

- What areas have been recently rezoned?
- Why have they been rezoned?
- Has there been recent multifamily construction?
- What is the town's planning and zoning department doing to encourage growth?
- Is the economic development office trying to improve the economy in that market? How are they doing that?
- What is the focus of the city? Expansion, redevelopment or restoration? What are their policies on crime prevention?

Understanding what this data means will guide you to select the best investment areas.

- How has the new multifamily construction affected vacancy rates and rents? When rents grow exponentially because of high demand, contractors respond in a knee-jerk manner and tend to over build. Once finished, older multifamily properties tend to suffer as tenants move over to the newer units and vacancies start increasing.
- Knowing the focus of your planning department will help you to be on the same page. If the trend is to restore and preserve historic buildings, then expect to receive favorable support if you invest in one. If their ten-year plan includes a new highway, what will happen to the properties just outside of the right-of-way? You are welcome to attend the planning and zoning meetings that are open to the public. It can be a great way to keep your finger on the pulse of your neighborhood.

Safety

Safety, crime and walkability are important factors to consider when you are investing in multifamily properties. Your tenants are going to be concerned about it, and that means that you need to consider it, as well.

A common trend we see with new investors is that they tend to gravitate to the cheapest rental properties. That is what I did when I started. While this can get your foot in the door, they are often located in high crime, war zones. These types of properties attract sub-par tenants and are considered high-risk investments, thus, the reason for the dirt-cheap prices.

I remember finding houses in Memphis that seemed too good to be true. I found 1,500 square foot, three bedroom, two bath houses for $1,500 to $3,500 each. I bought several in these war zones and I still regret it to this day.

Although I have owned properties in three states that were located in tough areas, I would advise the beginning investor to avoid war zones. I have had properties where the city literally had to block one end of the street to minimize and hamper drug traffic coming through. I had properties that became crack houses with people killed in and around them regularly.

These are incredibly time-intensive properties. You need to be prepared for constant tenant change-over, frequent calls from the neighbors, dealing with law enforcement and, at times, severe property damage. Dealing with that kind of stress is not necessary to make money. While it is true that you can make great cash flow on these tougher properties, you have to be ready for exponentially more work.

Where To Find The Data

Finding the data that you need to analyze the market area is easy. There are many sites that provide extensive, up-to-date information and localized data.

- BestPlaces.net
- Census.gov
- Geometrx.com
- City-Data.com
- SocialExplorer.com
- Costar.com
- Colliers.com

If you are looking for detailed crime and safety statistics, check out these sites:

- SpotCrime.com
- FamilyWatchDog.com
- NeighborhoodScout.com
- CrimeReports.com
- WalkScore.com

Please Note: We have a complete free downloadable list of every website resource listed in this book. (over 100 sites broken out by chapter available to you) at www.LifetimeCashFlowBook.com.

Most of these sites are free. Some, however, such as CoStar, require payment. If you can afford it, it is worth the price. The data you can find on these sites will help you get a clear picture of your target market(s) from an investor or developer's point of view. It will also help you identify sub-areas in your market area that have the greatest potential for income and value growth.

After you have done your research, I suggest you make a dated record of what you have found. In addition to the facts and data, write down your options and conclusions and why you made them. Not only will you start to build a database of historical data, but as you gain more experience in the market, you will be able to refine your criteria and draw even clearer conclusions off the same data.

For example, suppose 18 months from now you decide to buy another piece of investment real estate in that same sub-market. You can dig out your original research and the conclusions you made at that time and simply update the data using the same sources. Then you can ask yourself the following questions:

- Has there been any significant changes in the data?
- What could be the force behind these changes?
- Do these changes alter your original conclusions about that sub-market?
- Do you agree with all your initial conclusions? If not, why?
- Is this still a good investment area? Why?

Having the historical data will help you notice subtle market trends– some may indicate a good future and others indicate gray clouds brewing on the horizon. Both will impact how, when, and where you should invest in that market area.

Here's a story about evaluating a market. One of our students identified a 40-unit property in Eden, North Carolina. It was priced at $13,000 a door, which seemed like a great deal. The seller claimed the units were renting for $650 per month. The property was only 40% occupied, which was a big red flag.

When we started checking into the area, we found out the one major employer in town, a brewery, had recently closed. The area was severely depressed. We checked rentals on Craigslist and found three-bedroom houses renting for $395. We could have likely made the property work, but it would have taken a lot of work and management. We elected to back out of the deal.

Chapter 10
Locating Investment Properties

There are lots of different methods to locate great properties. In this chapter, we are going to break down some of the most common sources of good real estate investment opportunities. No doubt, as you get your feet wet in real estate, you will want to explore each one. But for now, let's look at the easiest way to jump in: Use a real estate broker.

Real Estate Brokers

In your quest to find great deals, working with real estate brokers should be first on your list. This is even more true if you are just getting into the investment property field. Frankly, there is no other member on your team that will help you more than your real estate broker. Real estate agents and brokers can be a great source of information about an area. Experienced brokers will always have the best market knowledge about an area, and will be connected in their markets. They can refer you to other members for your team. A solid relationship with a good broker can make you very wealthy.

How To Find And Develop Relationships With Brokers

Once you identify a market you want to invest in, you need to develop relationships with brokers that focus on that specific area. If you have ever searched for real estate brokers in your area, you may instantly feel overwhelmed. There are a lot of agents and brokers. So focus your attention on brokers that specialize in the type of multifamily properties you are targeting.

A good broker can make you very wealthy.

Brokers that are members of the following groups and associations have had additional education that hold their members to a higher degree of professionalism and ethics. You may want to look for brokers that are members of one or more of the following trade groups:

- IREM - The Institute of Real Estate Management www.irem.org
- BOMA - Building Owners and Managers Association www.boma.org
- NMHC - National Multi Housing Council www.nmhc.org

Another indication that they value education and hold themselves to a high standard is indicated by the designations behind their name. These designations and certifications indicate that they have increased their skills, proficiency and knowledge through the completion of required courses. The designation, I prefer, above all others is the CCIM. It is a challenging designation for a broker to obtain. This means the broker is super qualified and experienced.

CCIM - Certified Commercial Investment Member (www.ccim.com)

It can also be helpful to find brokers with whom you "click." This could create a lifelong relationship. It is not only a matter of qualifications, but also a need to be able to work together, communicate well, and think along the same lines.

We recommend that you ask your brokers to send you properties that have a value-add opportunity. It's always a great idea to let the broker know that you are always interested in any properties where a seller will offer seller financing.

There is something that you need to know about this new relationship: until you have actually closed on a property or two, none of the best brokers are going to take you seriously. They work on straight commission, and they won't make a dime until a property closes, no matter how much work they have done. They have all been burnt many times by buyers that have tied up a property for months and then failed to close.

Don't be surprised if some of the brokers you contact are leery of new investors and your newfound enthusiasm for real estate. They may even test you by sending you high-priced properties just to evaluate your experience. If this happens, it is important to let them know that this property doesn't meet your criteria and re-explain exactly what you are looking for. This will reaffirm you have clearly defined investment requirements, and it will help build your reputation. Ongoing, consistent communication is critical for broker relationships.

You are going to find out quickly that the attitudes of brokers with a new investor is going to vary, based on how hot the market is and how successful they are personally. When working in a hot market area or with a very successful commercial broker, it can be much harder for a new investor to get any attention. Even successful, multifamily property owners can have this happen when trying to buy A and B class assets.

These brokers are going to prefer to work with REITS or very experienced high rollers where they have already established a dependable working relationship. In a slow market, however, it will be easier to establish relationships with brokers. Also, brokers that are not quite as successful or new to the business will work with you. They will also be more receptive to listen to your requests for creative deals.

Much of the distrust real estate agents have with "investors" is that they come in every shade and color with many of them being too "shady" for comfort. If you burn the bridge of honesty, it is going to be a very hard bridge to rebuild.

What is more, the apartment business functions in a very small world. If you have chosen a well-respected, long-time real estate broker, they are going to have a really big network. If you burn your broker, he is going to let his network know, and you are going to find that one mistake will hang around your neck for a very long-time.

Trust me, you do not want to get a reputation of dishonesty in your marketplace. Be upfront with your brokers. Be honest about your level of experience. If you do not know something, do not be too proud to ask.

Finding Properties Online

You can find anything online, and good real estate deals are included in that list. There are numerous websites that list multifamily properties. Here are a few of the top ones I would recommend:

- LoopNet – The largest and most well-known (www.LoopNet.com)
- Commercial Investment Multiple Listing Service (www.CIMLS.com)
- City Feet (www.cityfeet.com)
- NAI Global–One of the world's largest databases (www.naiglobal.com)

Some really large real estate brokerages have their own websites.

- Marcus & Millichap (www.marcusmillichap.com)
- CBRE – A global real estate agency (www.CBRE.com)
- Cushman & Wakefield (www.cushmanwakefield.com)
- Coldwell Banker Commercial (www.cbcworldwide.com)

Most, if not all, of these properties are going to be listed with a real estate broker. In order to write an offer on one of these listings, you are going to have to go through a broker. You have several options:

- Submit the offer using the listing broker
- Submit the offer using an in-house broker
- Submit the offer using your broker

If a broker has given you the information on one of their off- market or pocket listings, I highly recommend you have them write the offer. They make more money that way and will be more inclined to send you more deals down the road. You may want to follow this plan for any listed property you encounter. When the broker writes the offer on their listing, it has a much better chance of being accepted because they have a relationship with the seller.

Buying Properties At Auction

Buying properties from an auction house can be an incredible way to find fantastic deals, but it is not for the faint of heart. These properties are always offered well below their actual market value and often well below the replacement cost in order to entice bidders to bid and then hopefully overbid.

There are some significant factors that you must consider before venturing into buying properties from an auction:

- Almost all properties are sold "As Is" and often without a due diligence period.
- Sellers can utilize the auction process to hide defects with the property.
- Auction houses typically do not allow any contingencies.
- You must have all the money in place before you bid.
- Financing these properties should already be lined up because you do not have much time to close if your bid is accepted.

We are going to give you some tips and suggestions on how to work with and find properties from auction houses. Make sure you understand the whole process, though, before you make a bid.

How To Get Started

There are lots of national auction companies. Some are local or state run and others are national companies. Here is a list of the top national companies:

- Auction.com now called Ten-X (www.ten-x.com/company/about/)
- Williams & Williams Real Estate Auctions (www.williamsauction.com)
- Hudson & Marshall (www.hudsonandmarshall.com)
- Albert Burney (www.albertburney.com)
- Comly Auctioneers & Appraisers (www.comly.com/home/)
- J P. King (www.jpking.com/landing/index.asp)
- John Roebuck Auctions (www.roebuckauctions.com)

I recommend registering with four or five of them along with whatever companies are running the local auctions.

How To Register With An Auction House

Before you can bid at an auction, you need to register. You can opt to register on-site the day of the auction. The registration period generally begins from two hours up to 30 minutes before the auction begins. The registration process will generally require one or two forms of identification (driver's license, passport, birth certificate, social security card, Department of Defense identification card, etc.). There is also a short registration form that will need to be completed.

You need to show proof that you have the funds for the mandatory deposit. This could be a credit or debit card, cashier's check, or cash. You may also need a proof of funds letter from your bank. Do not be surprised if the auction house requires proof of funds for each property you register for.

Many companies allow you to register online. The registration requirements are the same as mentioned above. Online registration will also give you access to the newest listings. I recommend you set up a separate email address to give them, because they will load you up with emails and spam.

The registered bidder is responsible for signing the purchase contract if they are the highest/winning bidder. They will also be required to close the transaction. If you ask an auctioneer what he thinks the property will sell for, expect that he will regularly understate the price to entice you to be in the room.

Types Of Auctions

Lately, auction houses have been jumping on the "virtual" band wagon. There are now three main types of auction execution and they include:

- **Onsite or Traditional Auction:** This is a typical auction. It is physically conducted either at the address of the property or another location.
- **Online Auction:** This is conducted like an onsite auction, but is held live online through a bidding software. Only registered bidders can participate.
- **Webcast Auction:** This is a combination of both. The live onsite auction is broadcast via webcam, allowing remote bidders to participate.

If you are unable to attend an auction, bidding can be done by proxy or absentee bids. When you place a proxy bid, the auctioneer will bid on your behalf. They will bid up to your highest bid amount. The proxy bid can be submitted via email, fax, mail or in-person depending on the auction company.

There are two categories of auctions: *reserve* and *absolute auctions.* A reserve auction has a minimum bid price for the transaction to close. If bidding does not exceed the minimum price, the seller is not obligated to sell. In a "Subject to Confirmation" auction, the seller can accept or reject the highest bid within a specified time after the auction.

An absolute auction means that the property will sell for whatever the highest bid price is with no minimum price contingencies.

Understanding The Risks

You can find some incredible deals at the auctions, but there is a level of risk that exceeds conventional real estate purchases. Here are some questions that new investors typically have about these risks.

Are Properties Typically Sold "As Is"?

Yes. You will need to perform all of your due diligence on the property before the auction date. The auction house will give you a package on the property, but it is up to you to check everything out as best you can.

Who Will I Be Bidding Against At The Auction?

You will be bidding against other purchasers and investors. Some will be new to the game, like you, and others will be very experienced.

If I Am The Highest Bidder, Will I Always Win?

If the end bid does not meet the seller's reserve price, the seller has the right to refuse the winning bid or negotiate with the highest bidder. If the auction is an "Absolute" or "Without Reserve" auction, any winning bid will be accepted, regardless of the amount. Each sale will be different, so make sure you know where you stand on this matter before bidding.

Will The Property Have Liens?

All properties sold through an auction house will have free and clear title. That means that there will be no liens, loans, or mortgages attached with the property.

What Kind Of Deed Will I Receive?

Auction houses (such as Auction.com) give you a Warranty Deed to the property. This will indicate that all prior liens have been cleared from the property.

Other auction houses may issue what would be the equivalent of a Quit Claim Deed (i.e. Special, Bargain and Sale, U.S. Marshall's, or Trustee Deed). Often these deeds will transfer with an owner's title insurance policy, though you may be required to pay for the policy.

It may be advisable to obtain Title Insurance, if it is not part of the closing, in case something was missed. This will ensure the investment is free of risks associated with a break in the chain of title.

When Do I Have To Pay?

All bidders must have a cashier's check or bank's proof of funds equivalent to the down payment. You will need to be able to pay the required deposit amount if that is part of their requirements. Many auctioneers just want to see that the deposit funds are available.

The deposit varies from auction house to auction house but will range between 5 to 25%. The purchase price will also include a Buyer's Premium, Buyer's Fee, or Auction Service Fee, which compensates the real estate broker and/or auctioneer. This fee will range from 5 to 10% of the highest bid. Any down payments made on a winning bid are non-refundable. If you are not the winning bid, the down payment will be returned if it was actually collected.

If the auction is online, some auction houses will allow up to two business days to transfer the deposit monies. Live on location auctions will require that the deposit be paid on the spot. Each auction house dictates when the transaction closes and the remainder of the purchase price must be paid by then. Most allow 30 days to close. Some require payment within two days after the auction has ended.

How Can I Pay For The Remainder?

You can pay using cash, credit card, cashier's check, wire transfer or company check (if it is accompanied by a bank letter guaranteeing availability of funds).

Auction House Financing: A few auction houses will also provide financing options, but all sales are made without any finance contingencies, so do not wait until you win to figure out financing. It is up to the bidder to have the financing lined up before the bidding begins.

Using Conventional Financing: Winning bidders can use bank financing on auction house sales, if they can close by the deadline. Since most conventional lenders cannot close in less than 30 days, many buyers use bridge or hard money loans and then convert to conventional as soon as possible.

If for some reason you are unable to obtain funding by the auction deadline, you will forfeit the property and your deposit. Do not let all the risks we listed above frighten you off. There are some great deals to be had if you are prepared.

How To Gain Experience At Auctions

A good way to get set up with an auction house is to pretend you are interested in a property that you will never buy. This way you can learn the process without actually buying. You will gain the experience without the risk. Plus, you will be able to see a real auction in action.

Some online auctions will give you the option to "View Only" so you can watch the auction. The view only option will not allow you to bid, but it is great way to get comfortable with the process.

What Happens At An Auction

Knowing what is going to happen during the auction process will help you to have more confidence. Auctions happen quickly, and a great investment opportunity can be lost in minutes due to nervousness and indecision. To help build your confidence, make sure to go to several auctions just as an observer.

Obtain A Bidder's Package

Each property will have a bidder's package. You will want to get your hands on it and start studying the deal. You will find that the package will typically be missing a lot of important and possibly vital facts about a property. These facts would likely be discovered if you had a reasonable due diligence period. As I mentioned, one reason why sellers use auctions is to hide problems that would have been discovered during a due diligence period. The rapid auction time table can make it a challenge to complete your research. Keep this in mind when examining a property. It is important to tread carefully.

Remember that auction properties are nearly always sold "As-Is." When you are evaluating one of these properties, it is critical that you do not just look at the purchase price. Do not forget that there will be closing costs and the auctioneer's fee.

There are more costs, however, that need to be considered. Though you have a limited due diligence period and limited information about the property, you will need to determine renovation/capital expenditure costs, operating and holding costs, and closing costs. While not knowing the exact condition of a property or having the fear of missing something important can cause inexperienced investors to shy away from the auction market, they can be an incredible opportunity for phenomenal deals.

Working With A Bank's REO Department

Once you have developed some experience and credibility, bank REO or "Real Estate Owned" departments can be an incredibly good source for deals. Lenders are in the business to make money. If they have an investment or loan that is underperforming, then they have a problem.

As I am sure you realize, if a borrower is unwilling or unable to catch up with their back payments, the bank will foreclose on the property and ultimately hold title to the real estate. The problem here is that lenders are not in the real estate business. Even more, they are definitely not in the property management business. They are in the paper money business. If it's not liquid, then they don't want it, no matter how good the income stream is or has the potential to be.

Once they have a clear title on a piece of real estate, they are going to want to clear it off their books as quickly as possible. If you can solve that problem by quickly purchasing it, then you may be able to become their go-to person when they have other real estate difficulties.

When a bank forecloses on a piece of real estate, they are in a particularly nice position to sell the property well below market value and/or offer attractive financing. Build those relationships with your local lenders. They can be incredibly lucrative.

Working Directly With The Property Owner

At times, the simpler method can be the best method. Making offers directly to property owners can bypass all the middlemen and allow you to negotiate one-on-one. These are usually the best deals and more often lend themselves to seller financing.

How To Find The Properties

Driving around in neighborhoods and looking for run-down properties can be a fantastic way to find deals. I call it "driving for dollars." Look for abandoned properties, rundown buildings, poorly maintained landscaping and exteriors. These properties indicate that either the owner doesn't care for the investment or they are tired of managing it.

If you find an apartment building that could possibly be a good investment opportunity, do not be afraid to approach a tenant and try to find out who owns the building. You can also locate who owns the property at the local property assessor's office. Then locate their phone number and give them a call.

Selecting What Size Property You Want To Target

It takes just as much time and work to research, negotiate and buy a larger property as it takes to buy a small one. In fact, I have found it is generally easier to buy a larger property. The growth and profit potential with larger properties is exponentially higher.

Larger property investments will regularly allow you to be more creative. It becomes easier to utilize seller participation to minimize down payments with larger properties.

It takes just as much time and work to research, negotiate & buy a larger property as it does to buy a small one.

How To Find The Owner

You can either go down to the county records office or search their database online. Most counties are now online and you can find all the property information, including assessor's cards, tax and sales records, and ownership information right there in the comfort of your office.

You want to locate the owner's information. Once you have their physical mailing address, you can send them letters as described in the next chapter.

If you do not have a specific property address, you can still utilize the county records to locate properties that fit a specific search parameter. For example, you can do a search query for properties with 4 units or more of which the owners have owned for over 20 years. You can then mail to that list.

There is one search parameter that seems to yield higher than average response rates. That is the out-of-state property owners. Out-of-state investments can be difficult to manage and are often a pain in the neck to property owners. This can be a great source of quality investment properties.

Chapter 11
Mailing Campaigns

Establishing a consistent and creative mailing campaign is an excellent way to locate great deals. There are a variety of reasons why an owner would be motivated to sell their investment properties:

- Bankruptcy
- Foreclosure
- Divorce
- Estate Sale
- Failing Health
- Retirement
- Financial Trouble
- Short Sales
- Inherited Property
- Lawsuits
- Management Problems
- Negative Cash Flow

Maybe they just don't want the property any longer. Regular and repeated mailings can catch a property owner during one of these events and facilitate a great deal on a property. The name of the game is solving the other person's problems. If you can solve their problem with a win-win solution, then it is always a home run.

The Timing

Many investors have failed to gain results from their mailing campaigns because they only mailed to the list once or twice. People's lives change and their circumstances can take a completely different turn from one year to the next. While they may not be interested in selling during the first mailing, their circumstances in life may have changed by your sixth mailing. If you stopped on the third contact, you would have missed out on a promising deal.

Some property owners may not even be thinking of selling but your contact lodges that idea and multiple mailings feed the thought. Property owners will often keep your mailing material in case they decide to sell down the road. When it comes time to sell, they will most likely pick the one that has contacted them the most often.

We have received calls from owners that we mailed to over a year previously.

An effective mailing campaign requires multiple mailings.

As just discussed, an effective mailing campaign requires multiple mailings. You need to get yourself in front of potentially motivated sellers at just the right time through a carefully targeted mailing campaign. This is a proven, effective technique to find great deals.

We mail to our out-of-state owners every three months. We mail to other multifamily owners every two months. Some of the best sellers to target are:

- Out-of-State Owners
- Owners dealing with evictions
- Owners that have owned their properties for a long time

Regularly sending out letters to your mailing list is perhaps the most expensive marketing option, but you can set your own budget. Mailing for deals has paid off for me multiple times.

Where To Get The Lists

There are many different ways to locate targeted mailing lists. Some lists will require that you purchase them. Others will simply require time and effort. Remember that cheaper and easier does not always equate to better.

List Brokers

There are plenty of list brokers that you can find on the internet. Some of these include:

- First American (www.firstam.com) – Yes, this is a title insurance company but they also have "property information on 99% of the U.S. housing stock," and they provide access to this data.
- Dunhill International List Co., Inc (www.dunhills.com) – This company offers mailing and email lists as well as printing and mailing service.

- Experian (http://www.experian.com/small-business/real-estate-leads.jsp) – This mainstream credit reporting agency has real estate information such as length of residence, home value, income, and even the owner's age.
- List Source (www.listsource.com/homepage/index.htm) – This real estate targeted mailing list source has targeted leads for foreclosure properties, properties with high equity, commercial properties, and absentee owners.
- DMDatabases (dmdatabases.com/databases/specialty-lists/real-estate-investors-email-list-mailing-list)–This company has been around for over 25 years and offers email and snail mail lists. They also have a real estate investor list that can be targeted to specific groups.
- US Lead List (usleadlist.com) – This company focuses specifically on motivated sellers, including investment property owners.

Rather than purchasing a broad list of all property owners within a zip code or market area, work to narrow down the list to a specific target audience. For example, all 10-20 unit buildings in a particular area whose owners live out of state and have owned the properties over 20 years. You will have a much higher response rate to your mailing. A broad mailing list may generate a response rate of only 1 or 2%, whereas a targeted list can create a response rate of up to 15%.

Assessor's Data

I personally believe in finding lists myself. I use data from the assessor's records. A problem with list databases is that they can quickly become out of date. It can be hard to verify the data. Creating a mailing list from assessment data takes some time, but in my opinion, it will give you a much higher response rate.

Most assessors are online these days. Start your search by locating the county in which your targeted market area is located. Within the county website, you will be able to connect to the assessor's database. Another option is to use their GIS system that is linked with the assessor's information. You can search by property address, choose properties off a parcel map, or search by owner name or property classification.

Not only will you be able to locate the owner's contact information but you can also learn the basics about the property including the purchase price (in some states), length of ownership, property size, type of construction, and recorded mortgages.

Working Around LLCs And Partnerships

In your research, you are going to find that many multifamily properties are titled in the name of LLCs or partnerships. Do not be intimidated by this.

One way to dramatically increase the effectiveness of mailing to LLCs and partnerships is to take some extra time and effort to locate a managing member and mail to the individual rather than the corporation.

It is pretty easy to locate this information. First, go to the Secretary of State's website to find information about the LLC. Most states will require that a corporation file with the Secretary of State. Other states may use the State Corporation Commission, Department of Commerce and Consumer Affairs, Department of Consumer and Regulatory Affairs or the Division of Corporations & Commercial Code. A quick Google search can help you to identify where you will find a corporation's Articles of Organization.

Second, you will need to locate the online business search section where you will type in the business name. This will bring up copies of filed Articles of Organization and annual reports. Within them you can find the names of one or more managing members. Be aware that some LLCs are managed by an attorney. You will want to contact an actual owner/member, not just the attorney/manager.

Once you have the name of a managing member or partner, you will need to track down their mailing address. Sometimes the address is right there in the corporate records, but if not, you can use online search engines for a basic search. Here are some sites that offer free searches:

- White Pages (www.whitepages.com)
- Yellow Pages (www.yp.com)
- Pipl (www.pipl.com)
- Zaba Search (www.zabasearch.com)

There are also paid skip trace type services that you can subscribe to and get much stronger and more accurate information on people. You could try the following paid services:

- Lexis Nexis (www.lexisnexis.com) – This may be overkill for a basic address search but it can be a good back pocket resource.
- LocatePlus (locateplus.com) – Unlimited searches can be completed for less than $2.00 a day. They have a monthly membership plan rather than a per search price. Their business search will also provide additional contact names and phone numbers.

- Experian (www.experian.com/small-business/skip-tracing-tools-software.jsp) – You can get mailing lists and people search at one site.
- TransUnion (tlo.com) –They offer pay-as-you-go plans for monthly a fee.

The Content

The more personal your mailing piece is, the more effective it will be. You want a balance of professionalism and personal touch.

The Letter

We personalize the letter inside with the client's name and address. We do not hand write the letter. It looks much more professional if it is typed on some sort of letterhead. You can use any word processing software to mail merge the owner's name, mailing address, property address and any other specific information you want to include.

I recommend that you put the address of the property that you are writing about within the first paragraph of the letter. This will help the person to know exactly what property you are referring to right from the start. I have also had very good success with letters that have a picture of my wife and I at the bottom or top of the letter.

It can sometimes be effective to have a headline on the top of your letter. Some effective headlines that I have used are:

- *Investor needs to purchase the property within the next 30 days*
- *Looking to buy multifamily properties in (city name)*
- *Is now a good time to sell your out-of-state property?*
- *I'd like to buy your property*
- *I am interested in buying your property*
- *We can save you hundreds of thousands in real estate taxes*

Your letter does not need to be lengthy. It is best to limit it to one page. You can talk about how much you like the area where the property is located. You can tell them that you are interested in their property and would like to discuss it with them.

Do not send exactly the same letter each time you mail something to that address. I think it is smart to change it up each time. Use a different color paper, send one with a picture, use different headlines or no headline at all.

Change the text of the letter to build on your previous mailings.

The Envelope

We hand address all of our envelopes. Okay, well, we personally do not address the envelope. We hire individuals through Craigslist (www. craigslist.org) to do it for us. There are also plenty of companies that can print your letter or postcard, address the envelope, and even mail it for you from your mailing list:

- Click2Mail (click2mail.com)
- ITI Direct Mail (www.letterprinting.net)
- Lob (lob.com)

Managing Your Listings And Mailings

The last few chapters have provided a lot of information about how to find properties and how to contact property owners and deal with brokers. But how do you manage all of that information? You could cover your desk with dozens of sticky notes or carry a yellow notepad with you everywhere you go. While some people function better with a paper-based system, I highly recommend that you utilize an electronic database.

You do not want to run your business in perpetual panic. So much time can be wasted looking for that little scrap of paper with the contact information on it from your last phone call. Life is just too busy to trust your memory to remember when to start the next mail campaign off the list you bought 6 months ago.

Much of this business is based on good communication. Every time you communicate with someone in your business, like a seller or broker, you will learn something. Instead of trusting all this spurious knowledge to memory, using some sort of customer relationship management software (CRM) can help you to build on these relationships that you have formed. It is important that you build and maintain a database that tracks all the communications and actions you have taken between your real estate agents, property owners and other investors. You must be able to track and follow up on every single lead whether that is a phone call, voicemail, email, referral, business card or conversation in the doctor's waiting room.

When it comes to utilizing a CRM system, we have chosen Really Simple System's software (www.reallysimplesystems.com). Their CRM software is built for small to medium sized businesses. It is a cloud-based system so you can access your information from anywhere and on any device that is connected to the internet.

They offer a free platform that you can use to track the names and contact information for all of the people to which you need to be in regular communication. When you are ready to take it up a notch, you can pay a small monthly fee (around $25 a month) and connect your contacts with their built-in email marketing software. It will manage your campaigns and has a bunch of other enhanced features. I find that this software more than takes care of all of my CRM needs.

There are a ton of other CRM choices out there. If you are a spreadsheet brain child, then feel free to design a Microsoft Excel spreadsheet that will do the trick. For the rest of us, we will skip reinventing the wheel and use an existing system. Some systems, like Really Simple Systems start out free and then offer membership to access their additional features. Here are some other CRM companies that offer really good real estate related software choices:

- Zoho CRM (www.zoho.com) - Communicate with leads via email, phone, chat and social media. It works with Google Apps and has a strong scheduler app as well.
- Highrise (highrisehq.com) – A very simple CRM software tool without the distracting bells and whistles.
- Realeflow (www.realeflow.com) – Specifically designed to fit the needs of real estate wholesalers and flippers and even includes a deal analyzer.
- FreedomSoft (freedomsoft.com) – Another system designed for real estate flippers. The whole system is nearly automated including lead databases, email campaigns and auto filled contracts.
- Podio (podio.com) – Completely customizable to manage your whole business, not just your leads. It works with Google Docs, DropBox and OneNote.

Repeated contact will imprint your identity in sellers' minds. If and when they are ready to sell, your system will already be set to handle it. The more your CRM can automate your contacts, the better your business will function.

No matter what CRM option you choose, you need to create a system to maximize its potential. Every lead, phone call, and contact needs to have a next action assigned to it and scheduled for completion.

It is a good business practice to establish a written system on what is the next step for different business scenarios:

- If a potential client calls you off a marketing piece, what will be your next step? When should it happen?
- If your real estate broker emails you a new listing that has potential, what are the steps you will initially do in your preliminary due diligence?
- If you are in a due diligence period on a property for which you have an accepted offer, what do you need to accomplish? When does it need to happen? Who do you need to call?

Make good use of your CRM. Make sure you consistently use it. But do not make the mistake of focusing too much on setting up the perfect software and the most detailed system and then forget that the end goal is to buy some income-producing real estate investments. Make the software work for you, instead of you working for the software.

Talking To Sellers E ectively

Humans are socially interactive creatures. Much of our conversations are not verbal at all. How we stand, our facial expressions, our gestures, and the tone of our voice can convey more than our words can communicate alone. When you meet with sellers, it can be very effective to match them as much as possible.

Matching the tone and speed of how the other party speaks is an effective way build rapport. You just need to be able to do this over the phone.

When a seller calls you from your marketing efforts or you speak to one from your outbound calling campaigns, there are some important things to remember:

- **Attitude is everything!** People like dealing with happy, positive people. Regardless how ludicrous their asking price, stay positive.
- **Smile.** They cannot see you, but you can hear a smile in another person's voice.
- **Relax.** It can be nerve racking to talk to a stranger over the phone. Remember, if you are nervous and you're the professional here, imagine how they feel. Work hard to help them to relax as well.

Sample Seller's Script

Having a script does not mean that you read it like a robot. You also don't want to barrage them with questions like an interrogation. Use this script as an outline to get the seller talking. Be willing to let them open up and talk. If you are willing to listen to them, they may be willing to listen to you as well.

"My name is _____ What is your name? What is your phone number in case I lose you? Do you mind if I ask you a few questions about your property?"

- *Where is your property located?*
- *How many units do you have there?*
- *What is your unit mix? How many one bedroom and two bedroom units do you have?*
- *What are the rental amounts?*
- *How many are occupied?*
- *Who pays the utilities, you or the tenants?*
- *How much do you owe on the property?*
- *Do you know if your loan is assumable?*
- *How much are you asking for the property?*
- *How soon are you looking to close? (If the seller refuses to answer, reply by saying, "I need to have some sort of an idea from you so that I'm not wasting our time when I come out to look at the property. I am sure you can understand.")*
- *If I would offer you all cash and close as quickly as absolutely possible, what would be the least amount that you would accept for the property?*
- *(Regardless of the answer) Is that the best you can do?*
- *When could I come by and see it with you?*

You want the seller to open up. Let them talk. Try to determine why they are selling. Do not assume that sales price is the highest concern. It may all have to do with timing. They may just be frustrated with handling the management. If you can encourage them to open up and reveal why they are considering selling, then you can gear your responses and subsequent offer to satisfying their need. If their need can be satisfied, then the price may not be such an issue.

Take a divorce forced sale, for example. The owner must sell whether or not they want. Splitting the price with the soon to be ex-spouse may be the least of their issues. He or she may just want to get the sale over and move on with their lives. If you can guarantee a quick sale, then your purchase price will look so much more appealing.

Make sure you are not pushy. You are looking for stable, profitable investments. You plan to hold on to the property, take care of it, and manage it well. Let the seller know that intention. Check your CRM database and/or do a quick search online to find out something about the property. If you can share something that you like about the property or create some commonality, you will create trust, reliability, and possibly an emotional connection with the seller.

Bonding With The Seller

Creating a bond with the seller can make a huge difference in your negotiations. If they like you, everything becomes easier. Don't be fake. If you are sincerely interested in them and can find some sort of commonality, it can pay huge dividends. I am not suggesting to take advantage of an elderly seller, but this is a proven method for influencing your transaction positively.

Here are some more revealing questions:

- Why are you selling?
- What is your ultimate goal?
- What are you going to do if the property doesn't sell?
- Have you tried to sell it before?
- What have you done to try to sell it?
- How long has it been on the market?
- Why do you think it hasn't sold?
- When do you need to close?
- When you sell, what do you plan to do with the proceeds?
- Have you thought about carrying back a note?

Negotiating For A Win-Win

The definition of a win-win negotiation is having a solution that leaves both people involved feeling as if they have won or at least gotten what they wanted.

Arriving at a win-win solution requires preparation and knowing what motivates the other side. People are not always focused on the things we think they are. We never know what the other side is thinking. Sometimes some gamesmanship is required. Preparation is almost always required.

Many great negotiators ask for something as a trade-off. Being sincere, open and honest when negotiating comes through to the other side.

Preparing For A Negotiation

It is important to prepare for negotiation. It is even more important to prepare in writing. Some questions to answer as part of this process include:

- What are your goals for this transaction?
- What do you think the other side wants?
- What is most important to them?
- What can you give up in exchange for things that you want?
- What do they want that you're okay giving up?
- How important is this deal?
- Will you have an ongoing relationship with this person after the deal has closed? (Such as if you utilize seller financing.)
- What are some of the possible outcomes from your negotiation?
- What does each party in the transaction expect?
- What happens to you if you're unsuccessful?
- What happens to the other side if you're unsuccessful in this negotiation?
- Who loses the most if this negotiation fails?
- Who has the most power in this negotiation?

If you will have an ongoing relationship with this person after the negotiation, seeking a win-win is critical. Seller financing will definitely create an ongoing relationship. Both people need to walk away feeling good about the transaction. Look to create a win/win negotiation strategy. Set a fair market price, and negotiate on non-monetary perks as a way to negotiate your way to your offer price.

Chapter 12
Real Estate Syndication

A syndicate is formed whenever a group of individuals, companies, corporations, or entities pool resources (time and/or money) to transact specific business or pursue or promote a shared interest. In the real estate context, syndication basically involves a promoter (issuer, manager, or syndicator) who contributes intellectual resources and finds a property to acquire for the group. The syndicator itself may consist of a joint venture LLC with multiple members working together as a management team to pool capital from passive investors.

The objective of the syndicate is to acquire, operate, improve and ultimately dispose of the property in order to generate a profit. A syndicate may be formed to buy a single property (specified offering) or the syndicator(s) may form a blind pool fund to acquire multiple properties using private investor funds.

Typically, the syndicator maintains management control over the property and passive investors. The upside of pooling equity is that a syndicator can fund a deal with funds from multiple investors for a property that would otherwise would be out of reach for an individual investor.

Some investors see the financial benefits of investing in real estate but do not want (1) to locate and research a good investment or (2) to manage the investment on a day-to-day basis. Investing in a real estate syndication is a hassle-free way for passive investors to benefit from an investment property without doing all the work themselves.

Historically, syndication has been done through word-of- mouth offers, limited by securities laws, to family and friends of the syndicator. A new popular method of marketing syndication to a wider audience is called crowd funding. With the help of the internet, a pool of unrelated investors is brought together. Experienced syndicators can use crowd funding platforms (companies that promote syndications to their groups of investors) or their own websites to promote their offerings. Because crowd funding can open up your deals to a larger pool of investors, you may be able to offer lower investment minimums.

Securities Law

Syndications are created so that a syndicator has a vehicle to legally ask private investors for money. If you are offering interests in a legal entity, such as an LLC, in exchange for an investor's money, you are selling "investment contracts." Investment contracts are defined as securities under state and federal laws. The US Securities and Exchange Commission (SEC) and 50 state securities agencies govern the sale of securities. Below are some basics of securities laws:

First, a syndicator can legally sell its own securities without having a securities license. Think of this like FSBO (For Sale By Owner) real estate; no license is required to sell your own real estate. For you to sell someone else's securities or for someone else to sell yours, a securities license is required.

Second, before a syndicator offers interests in an LLC to investors, the syndicator must either *"register"* the offering (i.e. go public; IPO) by getting it pre-approved by a securities regulatory agency (a long and expensive process) or qualify for an *"exemption"* from registration. Most syndicators (including giant hedge funds) choose to qualify for an exemption from registration rather than go public. If you are trying to close on a multifamily property within 90 days after you get it under contract, you will need to qualify for an exemption as you won't have time to register. You will need to hire a qualified securities attorney to determine the appropriate exemption for your deal and to draft the appropriate legal documents (i.e., your "securities offering").

Each exemption has a specific set of rules including such things as:

- Limits on the amount of money you can raise
- Risk disclosure requirements
- Minimum investor financial qualifications
- Whether or not you can advertise – most exemptions *do not allow* any form of advertising to the public – that means no securities offerings posted on websites, email blasts or standing in front of your real estate investment association meeting asking for money.

In all cases, when selling securities, a syndicator takes on fiduciary obligations to its investors. This means placing investor interests above their own. Further, a syndicator has an obligation to disclose "all material facts" related to the offering. They cannot present misleading information to investors. Criminal prosecution for fraudulent securities offerings does happen, so it is the syndicator's responsibility to ensure that its offering documents are correct.

Types Of Investors

A real estate syndication first needs a syndicator, comprised of one or more active real estate investors who joint venture to syndicate a deal. This individual or joint venture will find, acquire, and manage the real estate transaction. They are responsible for the due diligence during the purchase process. The other parties to syndication are the passive investors. A syndicator can be expected to contribute anywhere from 0 to 20% of the total equity needed to close on the deal. The investors will contribute the remaining equity. Each deal is different. Investor terms may vary according to the terms of the underlying real estate deal and the profits it is projected to generate from operations and from equity at sale.

When it comes to syndications, there are three investor classifications to know:

The Accredited Investor

An accredited investor must meet at least one of the following criteria:

- If single, they must earn a minimum of $200,000 per year and that income is expected to continue
- If married, they and their spouse combined must earn a minimum of $300,000 per year and that income is expected to continue; or
- Their net worth must be at least $1 million, not including the equity in their personal residence.

The Sophisticated Investor

This investor does not meet the qualifications of an accredited investor, but has some investment or business experience, or they can get assistance from their own financial advisor to evaluate an offering.

Everybody Else (Unaccredited)

If your potential investor does not qualify as an accredited or sophisticated investor, be very careful. They are the most risky investor you can put in your transaction. Depending on the securities exemption you select, you may not be able to include them in your offering. They usually require the most hand-holding.

It is important to know that managing your investors can actually end up being more work than managing your property investment.

In exchange for their capital investment, each of these investors will own a percentage of the company you form to buy the real estate. They are not typically involved; however, with acquiring the property, arranging for financing, or managing it. They may have a vote in major decisions involving the property.

Typical Exemptions

Now that you know typical investor qualifications, below is a summary of the types of federal exemptions you can select for your offering, if you syndicate:

- **Regulation D, Rule 506(b)**
    - No limit on the dollar amount you can raise
    - No limit on the number of accredited investors
    - Up to 35 sophisticated investors
    - Investors can self-certify their financial qualifications
    - No advertising or soliciting of the public allowed
    - Before you make an offer to invest, you must know an investor's financial qualifications and you must have a substantive, pre-existing relationship. This is the "family and friends exemption"; the offering must be transmitted by word of mouth,one-on-one.

- **Regulation D, Rule 506(c) – Crowd funding Exemption**
    - No limit on the dollar amount you can raise
    - No limit on the number of accredited investors
    - No sophisticated investors
    - Investors must be verified as accredited by a third party
    - Advertising or soliciting to the public is allowed as is internet advertising and holding seminars about your offering

The Structure Of A Syndication

Syndications are usually structured as an LLC or a Limited Partnership that is managed by another LLC acting as the LLC Manager or General Partner. It is very important to always use an attorney who specializes in corporate securities law (not real estate law) to prepare your offering documents. Over the past decade or so, there have been many fraudulent syndications that have cost investors hundreds of millions of dollars.

The following documents comprise your securities offering. Your attorney will prepare the first three with interaction from you:

- A Private Placement Memorandum (PPM) – this is the disclosure document that explains the risks of the investment, how the offering will be run, and provides information about the real estate.
- An LLC Operating or LP Partnership Agreement – this is the legal investment contract between the syndicator and the investors.
- A Subscription Agreement – where investors certify to the syndicator that they meet the financial qualifications and understand the risks.
- A Property Package for the property being considered – this is the document the syndicator prepares that describes the property itself, what they plan to do with it and projections of future earnings, expenses, and acquisition costs (so investors see where their money will be used).

The Operating or Partnership Agreement will set out distributions, voting rights, and the sponsor's rights to management fees. Each investor receives a return on their investment through rental income and property appreciation. Distributions of the rental income are generally made on a quarterly basis. The agreement may specify that the investor will receive a Preferred Return, which is usually about 5 to 10% of the initial money invested. The Return is paid on an annual basis, as long as the property earns enough to make the payouts. They can, typically, expect to receive a part of the capital gains if the property is sold. The investors will also share in the tax benefits of the property. The percentage of that benefit can be negotiated deal-by-deal, based on the needs of certain classes of investors.

Passive investors in an LLC or LP will typically provide all of the cash (minus any contributions by the syndicator) the syndicate needs to acquire the property. In exchange, they will receive 50-80% of the ownership interests in the company that will take title to the real estate.

The syndicator will keep the remaining interests in the company in exchange for its efforts in putting the deal together, conducting due diligence, arranging financing, and overseeing property operations. Instead of buying stock or shares in a corporation, investors will buy "units" or "interests"and become "members" in an LLC. Investors will purchase "limited partnership interests" and become a "limited partner" in an LP.

There may be one or more investor classes in either an LLC or LP, depending on what the syndicator decides to offer its investors. The syndicator typically keeps an ownership share of the company and an equivalent percentage of profits, subordinate to investors receiving their returns. Additionally, syndicators can earn certain fees, including such things as acquisition fees, asset management fees, refinance fees, disposition fees, loan guarantor fees and even real estate commissions, if licensed.

It is important to never accept an investment from an investor until the offering documents are complete and have been properly executed by the investor. Never co-mingle syndication funds between your personal funds or between other properties. Make sure that you open a separate bank account to manage the investment. This is very important.

Which Comes First?

Like the chicken versus the egg dilemma, many new investors wonder about which should come first – the property or the investors. While many "real estate experts" will advise to find the property first and then the investors will miraculously show up with money in hand, the reality can be much more stressful. Consider the following scenario:

An investor locates a 50-unit apartment building. It is in a great location, has low vacancy, and good income growth potential. The investor's offer of $2.5 million is accepted. He has agreed to close in 90 days. His lender is requiring a 70% loan-to-value, meaning that the investor needs to come up with $750,000, plus $200,000 for capital expenditures and operating capital. He has $150,000 to contribute, but needs to raise $800,000 more to close the deal.

The investor completes his 30 day due diligence, and the property still looks like a good investment. The clock is ticking. He only has 60 days to find enough investors to cover the $800,000 needed. If he does not get all his investors in place, the agreements signed and dated, and the closing completed in the next 60 days, he will lose his earnest money deposit.

This is a common mistake that new investors make. They start searching for investors after they have a deal under contract. This can create an "accept-anyone-with-money" situation that the buyer later regrets. To avoid this risk and the stress of missing the closing deadline and losing a great investment, you should develop a database of interested investors before putting an offer on an investment property. Once

To avoid risk and stress, secure your investors before putting an offer on a property.

you become a syndicator, you are in the marketing and fund-raising business. You have just added a new aspect to your real estate business. There are few single-member syndicators. Most have partners who share required tasks or they have paid staff to whom they can delegate. Being a syndicator is too big of a job for an individual to handle on their own.

The first step to finding a good investor is to write out your investment criteria. The next step is to create a list of potential investors. Network like crazy, and tell everybody you know what you're looking to do. We'll talk about an elevator pitch later on.

Once you have a pool of potential investors that agree with your investment criteria and have expressed interest, have your attorney start preparing the agreements. During this time, you can conduct your due diligence so your offering documents and due diligence are completed at the same time. While your potential investors are waiting for you to land a deal, keep them informed of your search and the results so they don't lose interest and invest somewhere else.

Chapter 13
Investors

Maybe you have heard people say, "If you find the deal, you'll find the money." That adage has worked well for me, but, as stated earlier, it can create stress when under a deadline to find equity to close a deal. Having a database of interested and pre-qualified investors can help alleviate that stress. Once you have a property under contract and are facing a looming closing deadline, you will be ready. A lot of people say to raise the money in advance. This can prove difficult until you have a sufficient track record as a syndicator and have successfully closed three or four deals.

I do not remember a time when we have had a better opportunity in the history of the United States in which to find private money. There are literally billions of dollars in investment capital on the sidelines looking for investment opportunities.

What An Investor Or Partner Can Bring To Your Deal

Depending on what you need to make this deal happen, you should look for active partners at the syndicator level (or management level) that can complement what you are bringing to the table. Defining the role of each partner and their contribution is a critical element of any effective partnership. There are several things that an investor or partner can bring to the table to help with the deal:

- They can bring money
- They could have the skills to help you work out the deal
- They can bring mentorship and expertise
- They can bring a track record
- They can bring credibility
- They can be a sponsor or loan guarantor for you if you're new (I will explain more later)

You are looking for partners that can bring one or more of the aforementioned items to the deal. Enthusiasm, desire, and ideas may be nice, but they should not be the strongest suit your partner holds. There is a lot of risk in any transaction.

Active Partners

An active partner will take an active interest in the management of your syndicate and the investment property. This may include overseeing the management of the property and tenants. It could also include financial or net worth contributions that help you obtain bank financing. An active partner will usually be involved in all major decisions regarding the investment.

You will always be an active partner. That being said, you may partner with other active partners who can enhance your ability to acquire institutional financing, find more deals, and/or enhance your ability to attract investors. All such partners will be decision-makers.

If you have partners, you will form a separate "management-level" LLC to serve as the LLC Manager or General Partner in your syndicate. Your management level LLC will earn the syndicator's equity and fees that can be shared with its members.

If your equity investor or partner will also be responsible for some of the tasks associated with a deal, make sure their tasks are clearly delineated in the management level operating agreement.

If your management level joint venture partners will also contribute capital, they should invest alongside your investors so their investment will receive the same return as the passive equity investors. In addition, as a member of the management level LLC, they will receive a portion of that LLC's earnings (equity distributions and fees).

Passive Investors

Passive investors may share in profits (equity investors) or may earn a fixed return on their investment (debt investors). Either may invest in your LLC or syndicate. Passive investors will not share in any of the day-to-day management decisions or property operations. Their duties are limited to providing capital for the purchase and acquisition costs.

Many investors prefer to be passive. They do not want the burden of management, but they do want to benefit from earning a better return on their money than is perhaps offered through other investment opportunities.

Remember that partners and investors, including passive ones, may also be able to provide valuable advice and mentorship in addition to their financial backing. They may have an extensive network or a strong credibility factor that they can use to strengthen your offer.

Here are some things to consider when you are seeking passive investors:

- Offer better returns if they will offer more funds
- Offer better returns if they will invest for longer
- Offer better returns if they allow the payments to accrue
- Offer better returns if they invest early

Passive Equity Investors

Passive equity investors invest money to acquire a percentage of the company you form to take title to real estate (your syndicate). Your equity investors will own a proportionate share of the equity in the investment. Because of their equity stake, they will be included in both the profits and the losses that the property generates, so you will have to account to them.

In exchange for their equity investment, the equity investor will receive a portion of the cash flow, appreciation, depreciation and other tax benefits based on their percentage of equity ownership. You may also structure your deal so that a particular class of equity investors gets a larger share of the tax benefits.

It's important to find out what your investors want when you first start talking about them investing with you. Do they want cash flow, equity or tax benefits? This will prevent you from wasting their time and yours. Doing this in advance of having a deal under contract will help you find and structure deals that are attractive to your investor pool.

Passive Debt Investors

A debt investor in your LLC may offer you their funds in exchange for a fixed return and a return of principal within a specified period of time. The fixed return is treated as a "preferred return," just like what you offered your equity investors. The debt investors get paid first, before the equity investors receive any returns. They get paid immediately after you pay the property operating expenses and any loan payments owed to the bank, if you have a bank loan.

A debt investment may have a shorter duration than your equity investors, requiring a refinance in order to pay them off, and they may require periodic reporting. Your debt investors may have the ability to take over management of the property if you fail to perform as agreed. If you perform as agreed, they simply get paid their money plus a fixed return. Eventually, after they get their principal back, plus the returns you offered, they relinquish their interests in the LLC.

Offering debt interests in an LLC is a useful tool for situations where you have a bank loan that prohibits subordinate debt. It can be used for seller financing in those situations. It can also be used for complex joint ventures with other private equity firms who might invest large sums of money in your deal as a single investor but want a preferred return over your syndicate investors.

Private Lenders

Private lenders will loan you money for your deals in exchange for a specified rate of return or interest rate. You have an obligation to pay back their investment plus interest, and there are usually remedies (such as foreclosure on a property) for default.

I had an elderly lady in Denver that loaned me money at a 10 to 12% interest rate as a hard money lender. After a few years, she had loaned me millions on deals. Though the interest rate was high, that relationship made me millions.

Private lenders fall into two categories:

- Hard money lenders hold themselves out as lender and dictate their terms to you
- Private lenders who are not in the hard money lending business, on the other hand, will accept the terms you offer them

Private lenders offer funds for the purchase or management of the investment. You give them a return of say 5 to 10% on their cash. They do not receive a percentage of the net profits so you don't have to account to them. They do not benefit from loss write-offs. They do not participate in the cash flow. They do not benefit if the equity or property value increases. They simply get paid their money with interest, and eventually, they get their principal back.

Payments on private loans can be made monthly, quarterly, annually, or you can have their interest accrue until a point in the future when the investment is refinanced or sold. Once the debt is paid off, their involvement in the deal is finished.

Their collateral for the loan is generally directly against the property in the form of a promissory note and mortgage or deed of trust (depending on in which state the property is). Private lenders should always be listed as a beneficiary to any property insurance policies. The term, payment schedule, and interest rate are all well-defined in advance.

Which Passive Investor Is Better?

Equity Investors

Pros	Cons
Can participate in all aspects of property ownership	Have limited voting rights on certain major decisions
Receives a return only on what the property generates	Invests in exchange for an equity position
Their investment is not secured by a promissory note	Will typically be more expensive, over the long run, than debt investors
It does not require payments on their equity deposit like a debt investor	
May require a lower rate of annual return than a debt partner	
Can pool several equity investors together	
Allows you to accept lenders as investors where a bank loan prohibits subordinate debt	

Debt Investors

Pros	Cons
Do not participate in profit allocation	Often require higher fixed returns than equity partners
Can be cheaper overall than equity partners	May be able to take over control of the investment and put themselves ahead of your syndicate if you don't perform as agreed
Can be paid off quite easily. (If there are no prepayment penalties.)	
Can be refinanced out of the deal	You must be able to pay off the principal upon maturity, which may be before you sell the investment property
Do not require equity	
Do not receive tax benefit allocations	
Do not receive a percentage of ownership	

Private Lenders

Pros	Cons
Do not participate in profit allocation	Often require higher fixed returns than equity partners
Can be cheaper overall than equity partners	Private Lenders can foreclose on the property if you default on the loan
Can be paid off quite easily. (If there are no prepayment penalties.)	
Can be refinanced out of the partnerships	You must be able to pay off the loan or principal upon maturity
Do not require equity	You may have required payments along the way, even if there is no cashflow
Do not receive tax benefit allocations	
Do not receive a percentage of ownership	

The Elevator Pitch

You need to develop an elevator pitch to tell the world what you're doing. An elevator pitch is something you can say clearly, concisely and quickly so that you could deliver it in an elevator. An effective elevator pitch requires forethought and preparation. This short, prepared speech explains *why* you are seeking an investment partner and the rewards they will receive if they accept.

An elevator pitch should spark interest in the investment or yourself. It should last no longer than an elevator ride of 30 to 60 seconds. It should be interesting, memorable, and to the point.

How To Create An Elevator Pitch

Here are three tips to help you create a spot-on elevator pitch:

Touch Their Emotions

Carefully construct your elevator pitch to touch an emotional cord. Are they frustrated by low returns on their investments? Do they long for a larger cash flow? Would they like to find an investment that will require little effort, provide good returns, and free up time to spend with family?

Leave A Carrot

Elevator pitches are not supposed to reveal all the details so don't pack too much into your speech. Never reveal anything that you don't want spread around. If they want to learn all the details, save it for an official lunch appointment.

Include A Call To Action

You're not talking just to fill time; you have an objective. By the time your 60 seconds is up, your prospective partner should know what the next step is. If you are looking for a financial partner, then communicate how much you want and how much skin you have in the game. If you want to discuss it in more detail, leave the door open for them to set up an appointment.

You should expect that it will take some time to get your pitch perfect. Practice it out loud. Pitch it to your spouse, your family, and your friends and gauge their reaction. You will know if your pitch is successful if they respond by asking you more questions. Keep practicing until you can rattle it off without thinking. Make it a part of you. Make it flow as easily as when someone asks you about your kids.

Sample Elevator Pitches

Here are some examples of elevator pitches I use to attract investment partners:

> *"I'm investing in real estate. I focus on multifamily properties like apartments and mobile home parks in strong growing markets. I focus on cash flow and appreciation. I'm getting deals with cash-on-cash returns of _____. Do you know anyone that might be interested in investing with me?"*

> *"I buy multifamily real estate like apartments and mobile home parks in strong markets. I only buy deals where I can add value and focus on cash flow. There are some fantastic deals out there with cash-on-cash returns of _____. I'm looking for partners to joint venture with me. Do you know anyone that might be interested?"*

You should not think that elevator pitches are only for investment partners. You can also use them on potential sellers and lenders. You can pitch it to anyone who asks you what you do for a living. You will find investment partners in the least likely spots, so be ready with your pitch all the time.

Who To Pitch To

You should always be talking about deals. It doesn't matter who they are. Do not assume that the guy who cuts your lawn doesn't have a nest egg tucked away with which he would love to make more money. Give him your elevator pitch, and you just might get some leads that turn out to be the best business opportunities you have ever come across.

The types of people you should be focusing on to locate debt and equity partners include:

- Financial planners
- Stockbrokers
- Insurance agents
- Accountants
- High net worth individuals, like doctors and dentists
- Mortgage brokers
- Real estate brokers
- and any one that will stand still long enough to hear your elevator pitch.

The great part of this whole process is that people with money usually keep friends that also have money. If their investment with you works out well, they will most likely talk about you to their friends. Over time, you will find yourself surrounded by a solid group of people who are willing to invest with you in future deals.

Ask them:

> *"What are you doing with your money? Would you like to a make return on it? Do you have any investments that are getting you at least a 15% return?"*

If the answer is, "No:"

> *"I am buying apartment buildings and mobile home parks in strong markets, and I occasionally borrow money from people like you to acquire and reposition them. Your funds are secured against the property and I pay interest. I also pay a few months' extra interest when I pay your loan off. I always use title companies, attorneys, and appraisers. All the transactions are fully documented."*

Remember that under SEC guidelines, you need to have a previous relationship with someone before you can pitch a deal. Once they have expressed any interest, you need to give them an executive summary of the deal. After they have had a few days to look over the summary, give them a call. Give them a firm date on which you expect to close. Get them to commit whether they are in or out. When they say they are in, immediately call your attorney and have the documents sent to your investor to sign.

Please Note: We have complete, free downloadable MS word copies of all of the scripts noted in this book as well as a list of every website resource listed in this book. (over 100 sites broken out by chapter available to you at www.LifetimeCashFlowBook.com.)

Put It In Writing

Never do business on a handshake. Investors and partners can wash their hands of the deal much too easily. Always have a comprehensive, specific, and well written-agreement between all of your partners and investors. The agreement should cover every possible scenario you and your attorney can think of.

Partnerships are great if you can connect with a like-minded partner who is equally focused and holds the same work ethic and business goals as you. It is even better when everyone completely understands their role and the returns they should expect. The problem is, in the real world, *Never do business without a signed agreement.* that does not always happen. This should help you understand how important it is to have a well-written partnership agreement that is clear, well-defined, and concise.

Put This In Every LLC Operating Agreement

There are a few items that need to be in every LLC operating agreement.

Specific Roles

Each member needs to know their role. Are they just a member or a managing member? Who has control and how much control do they have? Are they contributing equity or debt?

Disbursement Of Payments

When do members get paid: monthly, quarterly, or annually? What happens if the property has a negative return? Who contributes if there is a capital call? Who is entitled to compensation and distributions and how much? If a member withdraws from the agreement, will the ownership percentages change?

This needs to be clearly defined and should address different scenarios that can cause the dissolution of the LLC. When and under what circumstances can the LLC be dissolved? What would be the time line? Will the property need to be sold?

An unforeseen occurrence, such as the death of a member, can deprive the surviving members of their control when an involuntary partner, such as an heir or trustee, is thrust into the mix. Incorporate a buy-sell agreement within the operating agreement. It is a simple provision that identifies trigger events (including death, disability, voluntary or involuntary withdrawal, or bankruptcy) and then defines the subsequent action.

It is common to give the surviving members the first-right-of-refusal to buy out the other member's interest. The buy-sell agreement should set out the procedures and formulas that will be applied, including the time, valuation, and dispute resolution. This can keep the LLC functioning smoothly and reduce the involvement of strangers who know little to nothing of the investment.

Never get into a deal with a partner or investor without discussing all those different scenarios up front.

Avoid The Big Mistakes

It can be difficult to try to anticipate every kind of problem or situation that could arise in a partnership or syndication. Here are some problems and mistakes real estate owners can face when dealing with partners and investors.

Not Planning For What To Do If The Money Runs Out

An investment can seem so profitable on paper, but sometimes real life throws in some unexpected surprises. What will happen if additional funds are needed? Who decides how much is needed? What is the timing of additional cash pay-ins by the members? Can a member make a loan to the entity? If so, what would be the terms? What is the procedure if a member cannot contribute additional funds? Will it affect his equity interest?

Not Complying With Securities Laws

The SEC considers a money partner an investor if they are investing in a "security," if the investor/partner has:

- Been given a promise or an expectation of a return
- Invested money
- Relies on someone else's efforts to manage the investment

Any equity investor in your investment is subject to SEC rules. Once classified as an investor by the SEC, your partnership/investment now has to comply with SEC registration and reporting requirements. Your deal will need to comply with the SEC's Regulation D state-specific requirements.

You should consult with legal counsel and tax advisors prior to approaching potential investors to make sure whatever you do is well within federal and state laws. There are strict regulations relating to advertising. The SEC's regulations and requirements can be conflicting and confusing, and legal assistance is absolutely necessary to ensure legal compliance. Failing to comply can result in heavy fines and jail time.

How To Keep Your Investors Happy

Happy investors make good long-term investors. Investors who feel secure in their investment into your deals are going to be more likely to do a future deal or recommend you to their wealthy friends. There are a few practical things you can do that can keep your working investor relationships running smoothly.

Under Promise And Over Deliver

If you want to get your investment off to a great start, then let me share with you a secret: Under-promise and over-deliver. If you tell an investor that you expect to make a 15% return on your investment, but it only earns 12%, they will be disappointed. This could lead to problems and mistrust issues. If you told them, however, that you expect the property to make a 10% return but then it actually earns a 15% ROI, you have now cemented your business relationship. Guess what they will tell all their wealthy friends? You will have potential investors knocking at your door. When it comes time to pitch the deal, always quote less profit than what you expect.

Communicate Regularly

If you have a passive investor, one that does not involve themselves in the day-to-day operations, you need to keep them in the loop. When you are negotiating the terms of the investment, do not forget to ask your investor what level of communication they expect. Would they be satisfied by quarterly or even annual reports, or would they rather get them monthly?

Now that you know what level of communication they expect, you should plan to overperform. Give them updates regularly. Share a positive experience. If you know a large expense is coming in the next 6 months to a year, let them know ahead of time. If after 6 months it looks like the ROI is running higher than average, let them know. A quick phone call, email, or text message is all it takes to keep the lines of communication open.

If your investor calls or emails you, get back to them right away. Do not let 24 hours pass before you have satisfied their question. Never forget that they also have a shirt in the game. Even a passive investor is emotionally attached to the investment. Do everything in your power to maintain and build confidence in the investment and your ability to successfully manage it.

Chapter 14
Financing Your MultiFamily Deal

In reality, finding a deal is not all that hard. Finding the money to make the deal happen, is where the trouble lies for many investors. We are going to talk about some traditional methods of getting funding, some more creative options and some great options that many investors never consider. Each will have its pros and cons and must be carefully weighed against each investment opportunity.

Using A Self-Directed Retirement Account

Most people do not realize the IRS allows individuals to use their retirement plans as a medium to invest in real estate. This is typically done inside a self-directed retirement account with a proper custodian.

Traditional retirement accounts are typically held by a custodian. The custodian only allows approved stocks, bonds, mutual funds and Certificates of Deposit. A self-directed IRA or 401(k) is much broader and can be used to buy raw land, residential homes, commercial property, multifamily property, real estate notes, tax lien certificates and tax deeds.

There are 3 main types of self-directed retirement accounts that can be used to fund real estate investment purchases:

- Self-Directed IRA
- Self-Directed Roth IRA
- Solo 401(k)

Each account has their own specific guidelines and benefits, but all can be used to purchase real estate. Here is a summary of the differences between each account as they relate to real estate investments.

Self-Directed IRA

According to the Employee Retirement Income Security Act of 1974 (ERISA), the IRS will permit an investor to purchase almost any type of

99

real estate. When an individual contributes funds from their own pocket to a traditional IRA, the individual then gets state and federal tax deductions for the year contributions are made. The funds within the IRA are then invested and grow tax-deferred over the years as the IRA buys and sells investments. When money is drawn out of a traditional IRA by the IRA owner at retirement, the income is taxed at ordinary income tax rates.

- All income flows back into the IRA account
- Any expenses flow out of the IRA account
- A Limited Liability Company (LLC) can be created to hold the real estate investments and give greater control to the IRA owner
- Minimum distributions from the IRA are required at 70 and ½
- Penalty-free distributions are permitted once an individual attains age 59 and ½

Self-Directed Roth IRA

A Roth IRA is a newer account than the standard IRA and has a few key differences. A Roth IRA does not offer any tax breaks (i.e. deductions) when you contribute out of pocket, but the earnings and withdrawals at retirement time are tax-free. Contributions to Traditional IRAs avoid taxes going in, but you pay when coming out. Contributions to Roth IRAs, on the other hand, pay on income taxes going in, but you avoid taxes coming out. Roth IRAs do have income-eligibility restrictions in order to contribute.

- All income is tax-deferred
- Distributions are tax-free once an individual is over 59 and ½ and has had the Roth IRA for at least 5 years
- All income flows back into the IRA account
- All expenses are paid out of the IRA account
- A Limited Liability Company (LLC) can be created to hold the real estate investments and give greater control to the IRA owner
- No age-based required withdrawals
- Penalty-free distributions allowed at age 59 and ½
- Contributions can continue after the age of 70 and ½
- Beneficiaries do not owe income tax but may owe estate taxes

Individual 401(k)

This retirement account is a special vehicle designed for the self-employed, sole proprietors, or partnerships who have no employees who work over 1,000 hours a year. It is similar to a Traditional IRA and allows almost any type of real estate investment. It is also called a Solo 401(k). Similar to a traditional IRA, the Individual 401(k) allows for state and federal tax deductions for the year contributions are made.

- All income flows back into the account
- All expenses are paid out of the account
- Higher annual contribution limits than IRAs
- Can borrow up to $50,000 tax-free for any purpose at an interest rate that is at least prime +1%
- Does not require a Limited Liability Company (LLC) to be formed to gain greater control over the retirement funds
- All work done on the investment property must be performed by an unrelated third party

One nice benefit with this retirement account is that investment property can be purchased by taking out a loan from the 401(k). Since the retirement account does not own the real estate but is only the "lender," the income generated can stay outside of the account. The loan, however, cannot exceed 50% of the balance or $50,000, whichever is less. The loan is both tax-free and penalty-free and can be paid back over a five-year period.

Know This Before Using A Retirement Account

As tax guidelines and benefits change from year to year, it is highly recommended that you consult with a tax advisor to see if your existing retirement account qualifies or which account would be best for your investment goals. There are, however, a few points that you should be aware of when it comes to financing your investment with a retirement account.

The Income Is Locked

When it comes to using a self-directed retirement account, the investor must remember that the net operating income is locked inside the retirement account. If you decide to sell the investment, the proceeds from the sale must be returned to the IRA. While this option may not add anything to fatten your monthly pocket money, it is an excellent way to use investment real estate to build a retirement portfolio.

Transactions Must Be "Arm's Length"

The IRS has disqualified some individuals from participating in a transaction involving a self-directed retirement account. A "disqualified person" for a retirement account includes the account owner, their spouse, their parents and grandparents, their children and grandchildren, and spouses of children or grandchildren (son-in-law, daughter-in-law). The disqualified individuals also include any business or entity that is owned by one of the individuals, as well. That means that you cannot use your retirement account to buy your mom's house to use as a rental. You cannot use your retirement account to fund the purchase of an investment property owned by your son.

Using a retirement account to purchase investment properties is not limited to your account. An equity partner could fund a purchase with his or her personal, self-directed account. The legal entity holding the real estate can then make regular payments back to the retirement account. This can be done with a debt partner, as well. In these situations, the IRA is acting as the lender, rather than going to the corner bank. This can be another tidbit to include in your elevator pitch:

> *"Did you know that if you own a self-directed retirement account, you can lend money from it to finance a real estate transaction? The borrower, such as myself, would make regular scheduled payments at an attractive interest rate. It is a great way to quickly increase the value of your retirement account."*

Helping people to self-direct their IRA to invest in your transaction is an excellent way to find either debt or equity to complete your deals. There are trillions of dollars sitting in these retirement accounts or in an unpredictable stock market, gathering little to no interest. Educating potential investors about the benefits of utilizing those funds to get higher rates of returns can be a win-win for the both of you.

Help people to use their retirement account to invest in your property.

Bank Financing

Most of your transactions will require bank financing. Knowing what a lender expects or requires to approve a loan for your purchase will help make this process less intimidating and will help you to get approval faster.

Residential Vs Commercial Loans

Commercial loans are a whole different animal than residential funding.

Remember that you can qualify for a residential loan as long as the property has four residential units or less. If the property contains a mix of residential and commercial units or there are five or more rental units, you will need to obtain commercial financing.

There are several important differences between residential and commercial financing. Perhaps the largest difference is the term. A traditional residential mortgage is either 15 or 30 years. Most are based on a fixed interest rate. Commercial mortgages, however, will almost always carry a balloon payment within five to 10 years. The commercial loan will be amortized out 20 to 30 years, but the balance of the loan must be paid in full at the time of the balloon. Because most property owners are unable to pay the balloon payment from their own capital, they usually will need to refinance or sell the property.

While residential mortgages are almost entirely based on the borrower's credit rating and personal ability to pay, commercial loans rely heavily on the ability of the property to be a stable investment and produce cash flow. A lender needs to be absolutely sure that the property can support the debt service and meet all other expenses, while still producing a positive income stream.

The application process for a commercial loan is also more complex. You need to be prepared to present a professional loan package to the bank. You will need to prove your personal credit worthiness and financial stability of the business entity that owns the real estate. You will need to prove your past investment experience. The lender will carefully examine the performance of the real estate itself.

Commercial lenders also require a higher down payment amount. You should expect to pay 20 to 30% of the purchase price. This creates a lower loan-to-value (LTV) ratio than traditional residential loans.

If the property contains a mix of residential and commercial units or there are 5 or more units, you need commercial financing.

While residential mortgages are made to individuals, commercial real estate loans are often made to business entities, such as an LLC, trust, corporation, or partnership. As mentioned before, it is common for a buyer to place an investment property in an LLC. Because the LLC does not typically have an operating track record (such as two years of Profit and Loss Statements) nor a credit history, the lender will typically require that the principals or owners of the LLC guarantee the loan, even if the property is used as collateral.

Interest rates and loan fees are higher for commercial loans. Commercial loans will have more fees at closing than residential loans. Fees will include the loan application fee, legal fees, recording costs, real estate appraisal fee, other third party reports, and loan origination fees. These fees are considerably higher than residential loans. Costs for appraisals will be higher. You will likely need a Phase One Environmental Report to show the bank there are no environmental concerns with the property.

Recourse Vs Non-Recourse Loans

Most commercial loans are recourse loans. This is a type of loan that allows the lender to seek financial damages from the borrower and/or guarantor if the borrower defaults on the loan and the value of the property is insufficient to cover the remaining loan balance. A recourse loan allows the lender to go after the borrower's assets that were not used as collateral. They can bring legal action against the borrowers to garnish wages, levy bank accounts, and liquidate personal assets.

It is general practice that most lenders will require full personal recourse when making a commercial loan. This is especially true if you are using an LLC or other corporate shield. There are non-recourse loans available from big insurance companies and lenders that bundle and sell their loans on Wall Street. Commercial loans on a solid, stabilized, and performing asset qualify for non-recourse loans.

There are big advantages to having non-recourse debt. The biggest advantage is that the individuals are not personally liable. If the market tanks and vacancy rates skyrocket to the point that the loan goes into default, the lender will not come after personal assets. There are some disadvantages, however, to having a non-recourse loan. The biggest disadvantage is that the loans usually include some very stiff prepayment penalties called defeasance.

It should also be noted, however, that non-recourse loans often carry a "bad boy guarantee." Basically, this allows the lender to seek personal recourse if the borrower has committed fraud, misrepresentation or a criminal act that caused the loan to default.

Questions To Answer

Here are some important questions that you need answered by your lender before you apply for a commercial mortgage.

- What are the terms for repayment of the note?
- What interest rate can I expect to receive?
- Is the interest rate adjustable?
- Is the interest rate tied to an index? Which index?
- Are there any capital reserve requirements?
- When I accept your lender loan commitment do you charge a loan commitment fee?
- Are there any other fees that are due to the lender or loan broker when the transaction closes, like a loan funding fee?
- Is there an expense reimbursement commitment to the lender? When would it be due?
- Will I have to pay anything to the lender if the loan does not close?
- Are there any prepayment penalties for early repayment?
- Will the bank require you to open a checking account with them in order to qualify for the loan? If so, do they require a minimum balance maintained in the account?

While some lenders may offer a reduced interest rate to catch your eye, the closing costs can add thousands to the cost of the loan. Knowing all of the lender's fees upfront will help you to compare apples-to-apples when shopping lenders.

It is important to review your prospective lender's loan documents and any requirements as early in your process as possible. Their requirements should be well detailed in their loan commitment documents. If you cannot meet their requirements, it is important to know that as early as possible in your due diligence so you can seek other alternatives. This will also allow you to use your financing contingency to cancel the contract if necessary and get the return of your earnest money.

NOTE: It is important to remember that when you receive the term sheet from the lender, the terms can be negotiated. They are not cast in stone.

How The Loan Is Evaluated

The lender will run a credit report on all borrowers. The lender will also analyze all the financial statements and determine the net cash flow (NCF), the loan-to-value (LTV), and the debt service coverage ratio (DSCR).

The Net Operating Income

The net operating income reflects the income left over after all expenses, except the mortgage, have been paid. The gross income will include all sources of income generated by the property. This includes rent, tenant paid services, or any other sources of income such as laundry rental income.

Expenses will include fixed expenses, such as property taxes and insurance, and variable expenses, such as maintenance, owner paid utilities, and management fees. The difference between the annual income and expenses reflects the net operating income. There must be sufficient net operating income to cover the mortgage and the investor's target return or yield.

The Debt Service Coverage Ratio (DSCR)

The debt service coverage ratio (DSCR). more commonly known simply as the debt coverage ratio, reflects the annual net operating income (NOI) divided by the annual debt service. It measures the property's ability to service its debt.

For example, a property with an annual NOI of $125,000 and $85,000 in annual debt service would have a DSCR of 1.47. A debt service coverage ratio of less than one indicates a negative cash flow. For example, if the annual mortgage payment in this example was $139,000, the DSCR of .90 indicates there is only enough income to cover 90% of the mortgage payments. Most commercial lenders want properties to have a minimum debt coverage ratio of 1.25 to ensure adequate cash flow. Higher risk properties require higher DSCR ratios.

Lenders are not only going to look at the current income, but also any projected future income. This means that if you intend to increase the rents (whether through property improvement or tenant turn-over), make sure to include your projections and documentation for the increases with your financial statements.

Typical Lender Requirements

Here is a list of typical supporting documentation and forms that need to be completed during the commercial loan application process.

General Requirements

- Completed application form
- Copy of the Purchase Agreement
- Copy of any other agreements between you and the seller

Subject Property Information

- Profit & Loss Statements – two to five years
- Current Rent Roll including rent amounts, security deposits and lease expiration dates
- Information on the management company that you will be using
- Lease examples including new lease agreements and some current signed leases.
- Property Insurance Binder
- Property Tax statement
- Copy of any past appraisals (if available)
- Copy of any surveys (if available)
- Copy of any environmental reports (if available)

Personal or Corporate Information

- Tax returns – three to five years (Personal returns - two to three years)
- Personal financial statement
- Information about your experience

Borrower Information

- Prior management experience
- Prior and present properties owned
- Financial strength and stability of the borrower
- Financial strength and stability of any sponsors

A lender realizes that a profitable, cash-flowing property can be ruined by an inexperienced owner. A lender is going to want to see proof that you have experience in managing this type of investment. If this is your first large multifamily purchase, but you have successfully managed several smaller rentals, bring this information to the table. Show them your portfolio along with purchase dates, increases in income, current versus past vacancy rates, and any other information that shows you have the necessary experience.

If, on the other hand, you do not have management experience, the lender may require you to hire a licensed property manager for at least the first year. You may also see them require a few months of expenses set aside for this property.

Another way to build rapport with a lender, and increase the likelihood of getting loan approval, is to use a sponsor for your first couple of transactions. A sponsor is an experienced and financially strong real estate investor who has borrowed money in the past to purchase properties similar to the property you are trying to buy.

After Loan Approval the lender will likely require the following:

- Lender ordered appraisal
- Title search
- Credit check on borrower(s)
- Environmental verification

The lender may request a letter from your attorney stating that he or she has reviewed the lender's documents with you and that you fully understand them.

Loan Sponsors

When first starting out in multifamily real estate, it can be helpful to use a sponsor to help you get your first deal or two financed. A sponsor is an experienced and financially strong real estate investor who has borrowed money in the past to purchase properties similar to the property you are trying to buy.

A sponsor will sign on the loan with you to help you qualify for the transaction. A sponsor may or may not help you with the down payment. They can be someone who is on your investor list or someone you have a good rapport with.

To encourage a sponsor to back you up in the lending process, you will typically give them a percentage of the equity in the deal. Don't be afraid to give up larger pieces of your first deal or two to get them listed on your resume. That way you'll be able to sponsor yourself in future transactions.

Bridge Loans

Bridge loans are temporary, short-term loans designed to provide a mortgage solution during a less than desirable time period. They are also known as gap financing, swing loans, or interim financing. These loans are obtained to bridge between the purchase to a more stabilized setting to secure lower cost long-term financing with more desirable terms down the road. They can also be used to obtain financing when the borrower or the property would not qualify for traditional commercial financing. They are commonly utilized when a borrower needs to close on a transaction quickly. They are also very useful in taking an underperforming property and allowing time to reposition it to get better long-term financing.

Bridge Loans can be very good solutions for the following situations:

- Purchasing properties at auction
- Repositioning an unstabilized property (less than 80% occupied)
- Pre-Construction loan funding
- Foreclosure purchases
- The property does not qualify for a traditional commercial mortgage because:
  - Under construction/renovation
  - Lacks occupancy permits
  - Short-term high vacancy rates
- Borrower cannot qualify for a traditional commercial mortgage because of:
  - Strict lending standards
  - Owner is self-employed for less than 2 years.
  - Portfolio Reorganization
  - Funding is needed to cover the purchase of a new investment before the sale of a prior investment
  - Partner payout
  - Interim financing while refinancing multiple properties into a jumbo loan

Bridge loans are much more expensive than traditional commercial mortgages. They carry a higher interest rate, more points, and have higher closing costs. Because of the higher degree of risk, lenders usually require lower loan-to-value ratios and sometimes cross-collateralization. Interest rates can be 2 percentage points higher than traditional financing.

One positive feature is that there is less documentation and they are relatively quick to obtain. This can allow a purchaser to quickly close on a property and secure better long-term financing at a later date. These loans are often interest-only payments.

Bridge loan terms can be for as little as six months or up to five years. They are different from hard money loans in that they are funded by a bank or mortgage broker.

Mezzanine Loans

Borrowers often find the financing offered by a conventional lender to fall short of what is needed to sustain the investment. Borrowers looking to make up the shortfall may want to consider obtaining a mezzanine loan to fill the gap.

Mezzanine financing is a loan that gives the lender the right to convert to an ownership or equity interest in the company if the loan is not paid back in time or in full. It is subordinate to debt provided by senior lenders, such as banks. Mezzanine loans can be both debt and equity investments.

A mezzanine lender will want some sort of collateral. A second deed of trust is the most common. This would allow the mezzanine lender to foreclose on the property if the borrower defaults. It should be noted, however, that a primary lender will not always allow a loan in the second position. Thus, the most common form of collateral in a mezzanine loan is an assignment of partnership or LLC interest. If the borrower defaults, the mezzanine lender can take the borrower's ownership interest in the property. This would effectively obligate the mezzanine lender to assume the first mortgage. With a mezzanine loan, an intercreditor agreement is needed with the first mortgage lender.

Another form of collateral for a mezzanine loan is a cash flow note. This note is not recorded and typically does not need an intercreditor agreement with the first mortgage lender. It does; however, assign the cash flow from the property, as well as a percentage of proceeds from the sale, to the mezzanine lender.

A mezzanine loan can also be structured as an equity deal, creating a joint venture between the equity owner and the mezzanine lender. A partnership agreement is needed to address decision-making authority and what happens in the event of a default. If the property does not perform up to the expectations of the mezzanine investor, the owner runs the risk of losing control of the property.

Chapter 15
Easily Evaluating Properties

So, you think you have found a deal on a multifamily property?

Many deals will look fantastic when you first look at them, but just remember that not everything is always what it appears. That is why you do not want to judge a property too quickly.

There are two important components to every deal: finding out if you can increase the rents and if you can decrease the expenses. This will allow you to increase the overall profitability and thereby the value of the investment.

You are going to need time to accurately analyze the property and the possibility of improving its value. You also need time to study the property and area. This is why we have a due diligence period on a purchase contract. It gives you the time to research the property while holding the property for purchase.

Four Basic Components

There are four basic components or elements that make up every real estate investment opportunity. While completing the property prescreening, keep these elements in mind and try to define them, given the information and resources you have on hand.

- Cash
- Debt
- Time
- Risk

Cash is the amount of money you and your investors will be contributing to the deal. It reflects not only the down payment but will also include closing costs, loan costs, any required reserve funds, planned renovation costs, and immediate or emergency repairs.

Debt is the cost of the debt service. It must include consideration of the terms, amortization period, interest rate, points, balloon payment, and closing costs.

Time reflects several factors. It may include the time it takes to stabilize the property. If this is an under-performing property, it may take several months to get the occupancy rate up to market averages. The time factor also addresses the holding period. Is this going to be a short or long-term investment?

The risk factor can cover many different areas of an investment. It can factor in the current management and vacancy rate. It is affected by the surrounding market area and its future trends. Risk can include buying property farther away in a market area that you are less familiar with.

Risk also addresses the type of property. Earlier in this book we discussed the four different property types. These include:

- **Type A** – Properties that are defined as being a luxury property in a very good area and built within the past 10 years. They are constructed in the path of progress and expansion.
- **Type B** – These properties are typically in a good area and are recent construction for blue-collar and white-collar residents.
- **Type C** – These properties are in marginal blue-collar areas and are typically 30 to 35 or more years old. They suffer from deferred maintenance.
- **Type D** – These properties are typically known as "war zone" properties. They are in drug neighborhoods and have high tenant turn over. The properties are in fair to poor condition and are very management intensive.

Marginal properties in marginal areas are typically difficult to sell because they bring in marginal tenants. They have high tenant turnover, frequent unit damage and carry a high risk. Don't be afraid to pay more for properties in good areas, as long as the numbers make sense. Ideally we are looking for Type C properties in B market areas. These offer the best chance to add value without the risk associated with lower grade investments.

Any partners, whether they are debt or equity partners, will consider these four factors when making a decision. Analyzing these factors and summarizing your conclusions before meeting with investors or partners can have a positive impact on their decision.

The Initial Property PreScreening

Before you put an offer down on a property, you need to complete a pre-screening to determine whether or not this property has the potential to benefit your portfolio.

There are several things you need to learn about the property before you can make a purchase decision:

- The age of the property
- The condition of the property
- The location of the property
  - How is the area?
  - Where are the employment centers, schools, and support services in relationship to this investment?
  - What are the conditions of the surrounding properties?
  - Does this area have market appeal?
  - Is it in an emerging market?
  - Is the population and income growing in this area?
  - What is the unemployment rate for the area?
  - What is the occupancy rate of the property?
  - Is the property stabilized with at least 80% occupancy?
  - What is the vacancy rate for the area?
  - How does it compare to the subject property?
  - Is there an unusually high or low vacancy?
  - What could be the reason for the unusual vacancy?
  - How well is the property being managed?
  - How do the current rents compare to the market rents?
  - What is the expense ratio?
  - Is the expense ratio greater than 45 to 50% of the income?
  - Is there an obvious reason why the expenses are higher than average?
  - Is this a value-add or reposition opportunity?
  - Will the net operating income be sufficient to cover the anticipated debt service plus?

When you first find a deal, you are only going to have a limited amount of information. This is okay. It will help you make an initial decision to determine if you should spend more time examining the potential purchase. After you submit a Letter of Intent (LOI) and the contract, you will work to get as much due diligence time as you can.

You do not want to be rushed as you examine the property. You need time to analyze both the financial and physical condition of the subject property.

Calculating Debt Service

The financial statements will not include payments to cover debt service. A property which on the surface looks very profitable can quickly become an under-performing property when you factor in the debt service.

The debt coverage ratio (DCR), as described in the previous chapter, is an important calculation you will need to complete when evaluating the property. Typically, a lender's minimum guideline for the debt coverage ratio is 1.25%. If your DCR is higher than that, it will be viewed more favorably by the bank. It will be easier to get a loan, and the terms will be more desirable.

If you are getting traditional financing, a bank is going to look at the DCR. They will likely do what is called "stressing the loan." They will look at your loan with a higher interest rate or a dip in income to see what that does to the DCR. If the DCR looks bad as a result of their stress test, they will likely lower the loan amount. They will typically "stress" the loan upwards by one or two points. This is an important factor to consider since many loans carry a variable interest rate. The more equity you and your investors can put into a deal, the easier it will be to obtain financing.

If you have not made an appointment to talk to a loan officer already, you should make an appointment to see what kind of terms they can offer you. Because DCRs vary from one lender to the next, make sure when you leave, you know their DCR, 90-day interest rate range, loan to value, amortization period and the term. This will help you to calculate the possible debt service payment for a property you are considering.

Determining Market Risks

You will need to determine what the market rents are for the property you are considering. Even if all of the tenants are in a lease agreement, the agreements will expire. When they do, the gross income for the property could possibly increase, if they are brought to market rates.

There are several places you can look to help you determine market rent rates. The top online site is Apartments.com. You can simply put in the zip code of the property and check the area rental rates. You can also check the vacancy rate for the area. Just be sure you are checking apples to apples, be sure you are checking comparable properties with comparable amenities, etc.

Another online source is Craigslist (www.craigslist.org). This site will show you a wide variety of active, vacant apartments and houses in the area. One thing to remember while searching sites is to make sure you always compare apples to apples. If you have a two- bedroom apartment in a large complex, that is what you compare it to.

While it may not have pictures of the property, like Apartments.com, Craigslist will have plenty of information about the unit as well as contact information. We always mystery shop the comparable competition in the area to confirm rents and vacancy rates. If you call a property owner or their agent and they say the unit has already been rented, ask them if it was rented for the asking price.

Many property management companies post their listings online. Although you know I promote self-management, if you have a property management company working with some of your other properties in that market, give them a call to tell them what you are looking at. Since they have a possible new contract in their future, they will bend over backwards to get you whatever data you are searching for. A side perk is that management companies will sometimes bring you deals if you are loyal to them.

Another option is to consult with local real estate brokers. If they specialize in multifamily properties, they should have their finger on the pulse of the market. They will have the ability to pull up other comparable properties for both active and sold listings on the MLS to see what they are renting for.

Analyzing The Neighborhood

Location, location, location isn't just for single family homes, it also applies to multifamily properties. The ability to rent out the units will depend not only on the quality and condition of the units, but also their location and safety level. That is a major consideration of tenants.

How well do you know this neighborhood? When driving in an area, ask yourself the following questions:

- Would I want to live here?
- Would I want to work around here?
- Is public transportation available nearby?
- Would I feel safe collecting the rents?
- Is the property close to businesses and shopping?
- Where is the closest grocery store?
- Are there schools nearby?
- What is the rating of the schools?
- Are there recreational facilities nearby?

If you would not want to live or work there, then guess what? Your tenants will probably feel the same way. To get the true picture, get on the internet and go to Spotcrime.com. This will show you the police records for that area. If you want to really get the feel of a neighborhood, take a drive Saturday morning to see what people are doing in the neighborhood. Are they out walking their dogs and washing their cars, or are they grouped suspiciously on the street corners? Then, take a drive by the property after 10 o'clock at night. Do you have an uncontrollable urge to lock the doors and roll up the windows? Would you feel comfortable sitting in the neighborhood park?

Utilize Google Earth to see what is around the property. Getting a bird's eye view can really help see the big picture. Is it surrounded by residential homes, which is great, or are there a lot of industrial properties nearby, which is not so great? Does it look like a desirable area?

If you are doing your initial due diligence from your computer, click on the street in front of the property and look at the street view. How does the property look from the street? You can even "drive" down the street in Google Earth by clicking down the road and seeing what is around it. You can tell a lot about the area by what types of businesses you see on the streets surrounding the property. Also, checking out the photographs of the cars in the apartment's parking lot can be telling.

Looking Over The Financials

Ultimately, you need to research all of the possible expenses and verify the historical numbers. In the preliminary analysis, you will use the seller's financial information and make some assumptions.

Many investors use a rule of thumb when conducting a preliminary analysis of a possible investment property. The gross income is easy to verify with a copy of the rent roll. From there, subtract 50% of the gross annual income to reflect typical expenses. If you aren't going to self-manage, but plan to hire a property manager, subtract an additional 6 to 10%, depending on local PM rates.

This will give you a general idea of what you could expect for a Net Operating Income for the property. Remember, though, that this is not going to include the cost of your debt service. If you have a general idea of the terms, interest rate and loan amount, you can calculate the annual debt service payment and factor that in, as well. The remaining number is your profit before taxes.

Here is an example of a preliminary analysis:

25 UNIT APARTMENT BUILDING

Purchase Price		$1,550,000
Average Rent per Unit	$625	
Total Units	25	
Gross Monthly / Annual Income	$15,625	$187.500
Less Vacancy Rate	10%	-$18,750
NET ANNUAL INCOME		$168,750

	% of Rent	
Property Insurance	10%	$18,750
Property Taxes	10%	$18,750
Repairs & Maintenance	10%	$18,750
Utilities (Owner Paid)	5%	$9,375
Capital Reserve	5%	$9,375
Average Expense Ratio	40%	
TOTAL ANNUAL EXPENSES		$75,000
NET OPERATING INCOME		$93,750

DEBT SERVICE

Down Payment	30%	
Term	7 Years	
Amortization	30 Years	
Interest Rate	4.0%	
Monthly Payment	$5,179.96	
ANNUAL DEBT SERVICE		$62,159
ADJUSTED NOI - BEFORE TAX		$31,591

SUBJECT PROPERTY CAP RATE	6.0%
CASH ON CASH RETURN	20%
DEBT COVERAGE RATIO	1.508

The Income Statement

It is important to be skeptical about what you see on the seller's income statement. Sellers will regularly move operating expenses off the income statement to make their property look better. On the other hand, if you are presented with IRS tax returns, remember that when it comes to Uncle Sam, everyone wants to make it look like the property underperformed.

Take the time and effort to verify all the data on the income tax statement. Anticipate the most likely typical expenses you will incur if you purchased the property. Verify all historical numbers where possible. The following line items on a basic income statement can be verified:

- **Gross Rental Income:** Ask for a copy of the rent roll and the lease agreements
- **Property Taxes:** Based on the most likely purchase price, calculate the annual property taxes off of the most up-to-date millage rate. Be sure to estimate the new tax amount in your financial analysis
- **Property Insurance:** Call your insurance agent and get an estimate on the building insurance
- **Owner-Paid Utilities:** Ask for copies of the utility bills
- **Repairs:** Talk to the property owner and discuss the large repairs that he or she has completed over the past 5 years. Depending on the condition and effective age of the property, you can expect to spend between 5 to 10% of the gross income in annual repairs
- **Property Management:** What is the rate that your current property manager is charging?
- **Capital Reserves:** Allocate 5% of the gross income for large capital replacement expenses

Once you have verified the Income Statement, it is important to run side-by-side comparisons of what the present financial situation is with several what-if scenarios. What if you could increase the gross income by 5%? What if you could reduce the owner-paid utilities or yard maintenance costs?

You can then apply a cap rate and see what your what-if scenarios do to improve the market value of the property. It is important to be able to estimate a property's future value based on these assumptions before you buy. They can be useful when seeking financing, as well.

Chapter 16
Important Formulas

Investors will use several different financial formulas in order to analyze the profitability of an investment.

- Loan-to-Value (LTV) = Mortgage Amount ÷ Property Value
- Net Operating Income (NOI) = Gross Income – Operating Expenses
- Capitalization Rate (Cap) = NOI ÷ Property Value
- Cash-on-Cash Return (COC) = Adjusted Net Operating Income (NOI – Annual Debt Service) ÷ Initial Out-of-Pocket Cash Invested
- Operating Expense Ratio (OER) = Operating Expenses ÷ Gross Income
- Debt Service Coverage Ratio (DSCR) = NOI ÷ Debt Service Payment

Now, let us break each one of these formulas down step-by-step so you fully understand them. The better you understand these formulas, the easier it will be to analyze a potential investment and gauge whether or not it will meet your investment goals. It will also allow you to compare it to other investments to see if it is a superior, inferior, or an average investment. Fully understanding these will give you credibility with brokers, investors, and lenders.

Loan-To-Value- (LTV)=Mortgage Amount Property Value

The loan-to-value ratio is a measurement tool that is utilized by lending institutions to make sure the loan does not exceed their risk tolerance. Here is the LTV formula:

$$\text{Loan To Value} = \frac{\text{Mortgage Amount}}{\text{Property Value}}$$

An example of this formula would be if a property has a market value of $1,000,000 and it is financed with a $700,000 mortgage. The property has a loan-to-value of 70% ($700,000 Mortgage Amount ÷ $1,000,000 Property Value).

The LTV is simply the ratio of the total loan amount in relation to the value of the investment. Because lenders set their loan-to-value amounts, they can also take the liberty to decide what amount to use for the property value. For the most part, it will be the purchase price of the property.

Net Operating Income (NOI)

The NOI is by far the most important number when buying multifamily properties. It is the initial formula to gauge whether or not the property can produce a positive cash flow. If a property does not have the potential for sufficient NOI, all of the other formulas are basically meaningless. This is the formula with which you want to always start.

$$\frac{\text{Gross Income}}{- \text{ Operating Expenses}}$$
$$\text{Net Operating Income}$$

Now, the problem here is if your income statement is inaccurate, your NOI will not reflect the true financial condition of the property. This will affect the market value, the cash-on-cash return, and the debt service coverage ratio. Before you start calculating formulas, you must verify the income and expenses. This cannot be over emphasized.

If your income or expenses are off by only 10%, the property value will be off. You may wind up passing on buying a property that is, in actuality, very profitable. Or much worse, you could end up over paying for an under-performing property. So, please, take the time to verify the income and expenses. Many brokers will just present "proforma" numbers in their offering packages. They are effectively useless. You must have actual numbers.

You must verify the income and expenses.

Your ability to improve the Net Operating Income will have a direct impact on improving the property value. That is because the Capitalization Rate is directly linked to the NOI.

Capitalization Rate (Cap Rate)

$$\text{Capitalization Rate} = \frac{\text{Net Operating Income}}{\text{Property Market Value}}$$

The Cap Rate is the driving force behind income property valuation. It is a standardized assessment tool that investors use to measure the profitability of an investment in comparison with other investment properties.

The Cap Rate reflects the ratio between the Net Operating Income (NOI) and the market value of the subject property. If a multifamily property has a market value, or a purchase price, of $1,200,000 and has an NOI of $120,000 then the Cap Rate is 10% ($120,000 ÷ $1,200,000 = .10 or 10%).

What if the investor, while analyzing the profit and loss statement, realizes that he could cut expenses by 10% through better management? He would then have a $1.2M building producing $132,000 annually. This would increase the cap rate to 11% (($120,000 x 1.10) ÷ $1,200,000 = .11 or 11%). The higher the capitalization rate, the higher the return on the investment.

Factors That Effect The Capitalization Rate

There are many factors that can affect the capitalization rate.

- Overall market conditions
- Supply and demand
- Investment risk
- Property appreciation
- Location of the property in the market
- Level of property management
- Tax benefits associated with the property

What Does The Capitalization Rate Really Tell You?

It is one thing to know how to calculate the Cap Rate. It is another thing to know what this formula is actually telling you about the property. The capitalization rate identifies these three areas:

- *The Internal Rate of Return (IRR)* on an All-Cash Purchase. If the investor pays cash for the $1,200,000 property and it earns $120,000 annually, the investor has a cash-on-cash return of 10%.

- *Comparative Relationship to Other Investment Choices.* The cap rate is a tool for comparing investment choices. It factors in unique characteristics of each property through the NOI and compares it to the property value. The resulting cap rate can identify more

The higher the cap rate, the higher the return on the investment.

potentially profitable investments.

- *Risk Assessment.* The capitalization rate has a risk return buried in this rate. It would be incorrect to assume that just because one property has a cap rate of 10% and another similar property has a cap rate of 8%, the 10% rate is a better investment. Consider these two properties utilizing the 50% rule for expenses. Both have a market value of $1,200,000.

  - Class D – 30 Unit Multifamily Average Rent: $675 per unit. Gross Income: $243,000 Net Operating Income: $121,500 Capitalization Rate: 10%

  - Class B – 15 Unit Multifamily Average Rent: $1,100 per unit. Gross Income: $198,000 Net Operating Income $99,000 Capitalization Rate: 8.25%

Which property would you consider to be the less risky of the two investments? Obviously, the Class B apartment building. While the income is almost 20% less, which lowers the capitalization rate, the risk is much lower as well. So, as you can see, the cap rate also measures the risk attached to an investment, as well as, the return.

What Does The Capitalization Rate Not Tell You?

Because of the broad nature of the capitalization rate, there are several things that it cannot tell you. While the cap rate is a very valuable indicator of value and risk, it does not paint the whole picture. You need to understand that the cap rate is only a generalized indicator. Consider these factors:

- *An Investor's Return on a Financed Purchase.* The cap rate only measures the IRR on an investment if it is purchased cash. If the investor puts a down payment and finances the rest, the total capitalization rate reflects a split to include the return to the investor (cash-on-cash return) and the return to the lender. This split is called a Band of Investment. This means that if the investor will be obtaining a mortgage on the property, the cap rate does not accurately reflect the return on his invested money. You need the cash-on-cash formula for that.

- *Irregular Income.* The capitalization rate assumes that the income and the expenses remain constant. The cap rate should not be used for seasonal properties, un-stabilized investments, or properties with a variable income stream. The more complex Discounted Cash Flow analysis needs to be completed by a skilled professional.

- *The Effect Debt Service has on the Property's Cash Flow.* The calculation to determine the capitalization rate occurs before the annual debt service payments are subtracted from the cash flow. The reasoning behind this is that each investor requires different levels and amounts of financing. In order to compare apples to apples, financing cannot be factored into the cap rate. Just because a property has a good cap rate does not mean it can necessarily cash flow well when the debt service becomes a factor.

What Kinds Of Cap Rates Should I Be Looking For?

As we have discussed, there are many factors that can affect a capitalization rate. In addition, cap rates for certain property categories can vary from one market to the next. That being the case, however, there is a typical range for multifamily properties that you can use as a basic guide.

- Class A Properties: 4% to 7% Cap Rate
- Class B Properties: 7% to 8.5% Cap Rate
- Class C Properties: 8% to 12% Cap Rate
- Class D Properties: 12% or higher

How To Use A Cap Rate To Back Into A Value

Okay, so we have covered a lot of information here. Do you remember how to calculate the Capitalization Rate?

$$\text{Capitalization Rate} = \frac{\text{Net Operating Income}}{\text{Property Market Value}}$$

If you know the cap rate for the market area, you can back into information that is specific to the subject property. It can help you to set up investment guidelines that meet your purchase price.

For example, let's say the property owner has provided you a profit and loss statement. You have verified the numbers and determined the Net Operating Income to be $85,700. The cap rate for Class C multifamily properties in your area is 9.5%. With just those two pieces of information, you can calculate the market value on a property. Use the following formula:

$$\text{Property Market Value} = \frac{\text{Net Operating Income}}{\text{Capitalization Rate}}$$

You have a NOI of $85,700 divided by a cap rate of 9.5% (or .095.) This gives you the market value of the property as $902,105 or $902,000 when rounded. A purchase price within 5 percentage points from that number is market value.

Where do you get the market capitalization rate? Ask other investors, property managers, lenders, commercial real estate brokers and especially commercial real estate appraisers in that market. Write down figures along with the date and any other information they shared. In this way, you can build a database and take the average or median of the opinions that you have gathered.

You can also use the capitalization formula in another way. Assume you found a nice 25 unit Class C multifamily property you could purchase for $950,000. The market cap rate is 10%. What kind of income would this property need to generate in order to support both the property value and the cap rate? Easy.

$$Market\ Value\ \times\ Capitalization\ Rate\ =\ Net\ Operating\ Income$$

The property market value of $950,000 multiplied by the capitalization rate of .10 equals a net operating income of $95,000. When you analyze the income and expenses, the property needs to produce $95,000 of net income (not including mortgage payments) to sustain a cap rate of 10% and be worth $950,000.

Cash-On-Cash Return (CoC)

The formula used to calculate the return on a cash investment is a much better gauge of your actual return on the property. Remember, if you are getting financing, the cash-on-cash return also factors in your cost of debt service. The CoC formula calculates the return only on the out-of-pocket money that you and your investors have invested. It also accounts for the money spent on mortgage payments. This gives a more accurate picture of the property's rate of return to the investor.

To measure the return on your investment, you need to use the CoC formula

Here's an example: You purchase a Class C multifamily property for $1,000,000. You put down a 25% down payment equaling $250,000. The property was in rentable condition, so you did not have to make any repairs up front.

$$Cash\ on\ Cash\ Return\ =\ \frac{Initial\ Cash\ Investment}{(NOI - Debt\ Service)}$$

Your actual monetary investment is $250,000. The lender has invested the other $750,000. Let's say that the adjusted net operating income less the annual debt service payments, but before taxes, was $50,000. We can use the cash-on-cash formula to see what the $250,000 you spent out-of-pocket is earning you.

Applying this formula to the above example, you would be earning a 20% return on your cash investment ($50,000 Adjusted NOI ÷ $250,000 Initial Cash Investment = 20% Cash-on-Cash Return). A 20% return is very attractive. But consider the cap rate on this property. Let's assume that the borrower finances $750,000 at a 4% interest rate, amortized over 30 years with a 10 year balloon on a monthly payment schedule. Over the course of the year, the investor will pay $42,967 in mortgage payments. If we add that back into the adjusted NOI ($50,000) that was used in the Cash-on-Cash formula, the Net Operating Income would be $92,967 ($42,967 + $50,000).

Using the cap rate formula of Net Operating Income ÷ Property Value = Capitalization Rate, the cap rate on this property is only 9.2% ($92,967 NOI ÷ $1,000,000 Property Value = 0.092 or 9.2%).

A Class C investment with a 9.2% cap rate is well within the average range of 8 to 12%. But the reality is that the investor is earning much more than 9.2% off the investment. Since he purchased the property using other people's money (bank funds), he was able to get a much higher return on his investment. Now, if the investor paid the full $1,000,000 cash, his return would be only 9.2%.

When analyzing an income producing property, you will want to use the Capitalization Rate formula to compare different types of investments. It measures the cost effectiveness of an investment. If you want to measure the return on your investment, you will need to use the Cash-on-Cash formula. It measures the profitability of the actual cash investment that was made by the investor into the property. Remember, unlike the capitalization rate, the cash-on-cash formula takes into consideration debt service.

Operating Expense Ratio (OER)

The operating expense ratio is an easy formula that measures the relationship between the expenses and the gross income. The operating expense ratio is calculated by using the following formula:

$$\text{Operating Expense Ratio } = \frac{\text{Operating Expenses}}{\text{Gross Income}}$$

This formula measures how much of the gross rental income is needed to cover all of the operating expenses including property taxes and insurance, maintenance, repairs, property management fees, utilities, and capital reserves.

An example of this formula in action would be if your rental property was producing a gross income of $100,000 and your operating expenses over a one year period amounted to $55,000, then your operating expense ratio would be 55% ($55,000 Operating Expenses ÷ $100,000 Gross Income =.55).

Are you familiar with the 50% expense ratio rule that is used by seasoned investors? It is based on the idea that, as a rule of thumb, a multifamily income property will spend 50% of the gross income on expenses. This 50% includes the vacancy rate but does not include property management costs (since not all investors utilize this service) but all are affected by vacancy. In reality, the 50% rule is simply a market driven Operating Expense Ratio. It is frequently used as a quick measurement of the cash flow to see if enough income remains to cover the debt service and investor returns.

Debt Service Coverage

We have discussed the debt service coverage ratio in a previous chapter. But, as a review, this formula is calculated as follows:

Debt Service Coverage Ratio = NOI ÷ Debt Service Payment

This formula is used by lenders as a gauge of the property's ability to meet the mortgage payments utilizing the cash flow from its operation. Lenders want to see a property have at least 20 to 25% of the net operating income left over after paying the mortgage. This means that to qualify for a commercial mortgage, you will generally need to find a property that has a debt service coverage ratio of at least 1.20-1.25.

A DSCR of less than 1 means the investment has a negative cash flow. A DSCR of .92 would indicate there is only enough net operating income to cover 92% of the annual debt payments. This means the investors would need to come up with the other 8% out of their own finances.

An example of the DSCR would be an investment property that is being offered for sale at a price of $950,000. It generates a gross income of $100,000. The annual expenses total $55,000. The Net Operating Income is $45,000. With the annual mortgage payments totaling $40,900, the DSCR is 1.22. Let's say that you make an offer on the property that is 7% below the asking price. The debt service ratio is now 1.32. This indicates that the investor will have 32% of his profits left over after paying all of his operating expenses and debt service.

The debt service coverage ratio will take into consideration all debt obligations. Using the DSCR formula when analyzing a potential investment purchase will help to quantify the cash flow of the property and can help to see if you meet minimum lender qualifications.

Hidden Opportunities

Always take time to look for hidden opportunities on the property. What would make up a hidden opportunity? Is there extra buildable land? Could rentable storage units be placed on the property? I once purchased an 88-unit apartment complex in Punta Gorda, Florida that had an additional 5 acres that could be used to build more apartments. That was a huge win when buying that complex.

If the property has extra land, who owns the property next door? Does combining the properties make sense? Could the combination of nearby properties increase the worth and developmental potential of the existing property?

Another option is to consider opportunities within the structure itself. Does the property have laundry facilities? If not, is there an area where they could be installed? Does the property have covered parking? Would providing such justify an increase of rent? If so, how much and how long would it take to recoup the investment cost? Is there a clubhouse that is not being used to its potential that could be re-purposed for something that generates income? I have a friend that just bought 100 units in Tampa, and he is turning his clubhouse into three additional rental units for a big swing in NOI and value.

Property Evaluation Software

When you decide to pursue larger properties or more of them, you will need to either customize an Excel spreadsheet or get your hands on some financial property evaluation software. There are plenty of different types of evaluation software packages out there. Here are a few:

- RealData (www.realdata.com) – This software has two versions: Express for smaller portfolios and Professional for income properties, including hotels. The Professional edition can compare individual units and combine income from different property types. There are separate product lines for Windows and Mac, and they offer support for both.

- REI Wise (www.reiwise.com/index.aspx) – This cloud-based software is available by subscription. It includes investment, leasing, and financial modeling, as well as marketing tools. This software is designed for property investors. It includes a transaction platform with a virtual deal room and document center to help make transactions easier.

- ProAPOD (www.proapod.com) – This property analysis software comes in 3 versions that can help beginner investors all the way up to more experienced investors with large portfolios and multiple building investments. The purchase of this software includes access to the online iCalculator for investments, cash flows, time value analysis, and more.

- CRE Model (www.cremodel.com) – This affordable property investment software models the most common investment metrics for small to medium-sized investors. Calculations include Return on Investment (ROI), leveraged Internal Rates of Return (IRR), and cash-on-cash returns. It can work with Windows or Mac.

- RealBench(www.realbench.net)– By evaluating customizable benchmarks, like gross rent multipliers and debt coverage ratios, it can assist in making better investment decisions. It features a multi-property comparison dashboard to analyze several properties at once.

- PlanEASe (www.planease.com/default.aspx) – It was created as a commercial property software suite for financial analysis and cash flow projections. It is available for Windows and offers cloud versions. It contains a comprehensive management of multi-unit residential and office properties. Extensions can be added to the base module to include graphics, reporting, and the ability to combine files for portfolio analysis.

- The Analyst PRO (blyn.cc) – This company offers commercial analysis software through their app. The app bundles financial calculators, investment analysis tools, and PDF reporting. Features include an amortization calculator and property distance measuring.

- Argus Software (www.argussoftware.com/en/default.aspx) – This is an enterprise-level software package for commercial real estate companies. Functions include asset, portfolio, and lease management, as well as valuation, extensive budgeting, and collaboration capabilities to support team work flows.

The pre-screening process is an important part of the property analysis. Before you rush to put an offer on a seemingly great deal, take some time to pre-screen the property. You do not want to unnecessarily tie up earnest money with offers that turn out to be non-cash flowing properties and thereby upset brokers. Do your best to evaluate the property before you submit an offer.

We offer some easy to use and very economical Deal Evaluator Software in conjunction with our online course. It allows you to quickly analyze prospective deals and do "what if" scenarios to evaluate a property from all angles.

Chapter 17
Preparing And Presenting
O ers

Once the preliminary analysis of the property has been completed and the results indicate that this investment has the potential to 1) have steady positive cash flow, 2) maintain a stable to increasing property value and 3) meet the investor's return criteria, it is now time to submit an offer. When it comes to preparing and presenting an offer, there is much more to the process than simply calling up your real estate broker and giving them your price and away it flies. This chapter is going to break down the mechanics of preparing and presenting your offers.

Try To Learn The Motivation

Purchasing an investment property is more than just submitting an offer. It is more than simply agreeing on a price. Buying real estate is all about negotiation. It is a meeting of the minds; a coming to a mutually acceptable agreement. When presenting offers, remember that everything is a negotiation.

When you, as the buyer, can understand the motivation behind why the seller is selling, then you have the power to negotiate in a way that goes way beyond the sales price. The people we are dealing with are not always focused on what we think they are. We have to try to get into their minds and figure out what is the driving force that has motivated the sale. We have to figure out what it is they want to accomplish through the sale of their property. While we as the buyers are concerned with price, that may not always be the seller's primary motivation.

Imagine a seller who is nearing retirement. He owns several multifamily properties that are doing well, but he would like to shift from management intensive multifamily into properties that have investment-grade tenants on absolute net leases. He has found an ideal investment but needs to act on it quickly to secure the deal. What is this seller's motivation? Is it price or time? While he would ideally like to get the best price possible, the time factor is more of an issue here. How can that work to your advantage?

Everything is a negotiation

When you can understand the motivation behind a seller, you are in a better position to negotiate a deal that caters to their needs. In this case, the savvy investor offers a discounted purchase price with an all - cash closing in 30 days. Though the buyer knows that he cannot get conventional financing that quick, he is confident that he could find a bridge or hard money lender to facilitate the rapid purchase. The discounted sales price will more than compensate for the costs of the short-term loan until more conventional financing can be obtained. The seller quickly accepts the offer and everyone wins.

Consider another common scenario. The seller owns a large portfolio. Over half of his portfolio is listed for sale. The buyer learns that the seller is tired of managing real estate and wants to shift his portfolio into other investments. The buyer suggests that instead of being hit with huge capital gains tax off the sales of all of his real estate, he recommends owner financing. The monthly payments would provide the seller cash flow without incurring a hard hitting tax bill. The buyer and seller negotiate the terms of the seller financing, and the deal is accepted. Because the buyer took the time to learn the motivation behind the sale, he was able to present an offer that appealed to the seller, while negotiating a very attractive purchase price for himself.

The Purchase Price

When an inexperienced investor completes a preliminary analysis of the property, he may find himself making a very common mistake. The investor has analyzed what he can do with the property. Perhaps the property is currently underperforming due to high vacancy and poor management. The investor knows that within six months he has the ability to increase the monthly gross income by 18%. While that is great, it should not affect your purchase price.

We base our offer on how the property is performing today and subsequently what it is worth today, not what it will be worth in the future. You do not need to compensate the current owner for the improvements you make to the property in the future. The current market value of the property needs to be based on the current NOI.

Now, on the other side of this coin, those projections will be useful when you go for bank financing. A lender is going to factor in your experience, management, and ability to stabilize the property.

The point that we are trying to makehere is to be careful when submitting a purchase price. Make sure that it reflects the

Base your offer on what it is worth today, not what it will be worth in the future.

value of the property on that day. If it is an income-producing investment property, then the value of the property should be based off the current income, not the future potential. If you are looking into a property that has special features, developmental potential, or any other unusual characteristics, take the time to get advice from someone who has the experience and qualifications to help you determine the correct purchase price. It may require that you meet with the zoning administrator or hire the services of a commercial appraiser.

Do not let a broker tell you that you're crazy for evaluating a building based on actual numbers rather than proforma numbers. Don't be afraid to let them know you have evaluated the property and this is what you think it is worth. The listing broker would love to have you overpay for the property. Do not let them intimidate you. If you have carefully done your homework, you can feel confident about your valuation.

There are some investors, and their gurus, who will tell you that everything is negotiable after submitting the offer. While that may be true, you take the risk of killing the deal by dragging everyone back to the negotiating table. Do your due diligence prior to submitting the offer. That being said, if the seller made a representation about the property that you determine to be inaccurate through your due diligence, by all means "re-trade" or renegotiate.

The Letter Of Intent

The letter of intent (LOI) is a document we use to begin the negotiations on a property. The LOI is just that; it shows your intent and desire to purchase the property. Before you prepare a written contract, submit a letter of intent first. This will help you to know if you and the seller are on the same page. It will save money on unnecessary legal fees for contract preparation.

The LOI is typically only two to four pages long. It is a nonbinding agreement. It is fairly simplistic in outlining the major deal points, such as the price, terms, and other property specific factors. The actual purchase and sales contract will contain all the legal language and details. For now, you just want to see if the seller is willing to consider the offer on these terms.

At a minimum, the LOI will contain the following information:

- Name of the property, if it has one
- Property address
- Property tax identification number
- Legal description of the property

- Purchase price
- Earnest money deposit amount
- Payment arrangements, such as cash, mortgage, seller financing, etc.
- Projected closing date
- Terms and time frames for your due diligence
- Who will create the contract

Any important, non-standard terms or large requests that you are making should also be stated in the LOI. It would include items such as owner financing, closing costs, which ones are to be paid by the seller, and who obtains and pays for any environmental reports or other similar items. Get these negotiation points done at the LOI stage before you waste money on creating a lengthy contract. To give you a general idea as to the verbiage of the LOI, here is a sample to which you can refer.

LETTER OF INTENT

<Name of Broker or Seller>   Date: *<Date>*

<Address>

RE: Letter of Intent for the property located at *<property's legal address and parcel number>* (the "Property")

Dear *<Name of Broker or Seller>:*

This letter follows up on our recent discussions regarding the Property (as defined above). This is a letter of intent only and, except as provided otherwise herein, neither party will be bound until a mutually agreeable purchase and sales agreement (the "Purchase Agreement") has been executed by both parties. Subject to the foregoing, Buyer (as defined below) would be willing to enter into a Purchase Agreement with Seller (as defined below) that includes the following terms and condition:

1. Buyer: *<Name of buying LLC>* and/or assigns

   ("Buyer")

2. Seller: *<Name of seller>(*"Seller")

3. Price: *<Purchase Price>*

4. Down Payment: *<Down Payment Amount>*

5 Payment Terms: Financed amount to be *<Mortgage Amount>*, *<#>* year amortization, *<#>%* interest, *<#>* year balloon with *(#) #* year balloon extensions.

6. Escrow: Escrow to be opened at *<Name of Attorney or Title Company> ("Escrow Company"),* upon both parties' execution ("Mutual Execution") of a Purchase Agreement.

7. Closing: The transaction will close at *<Name of Attorney or Title Company>* within *<fifteen>* days *(15)* days after the end of the Contingency Period (as defined below), unless the transaction is terminated prior to such time. The Property will be conveyed by statutory warranty deed, subject to exceptions

agreed upon by Buyer and Seller (the "Permitted Exceptions") prior to the end of the Contingency Period. At closing, Seller will assign and Buyer will assume all leases and contracts approved by Buyer related to the Property.

8. Conditions for the Benefit of Buyer/Contingency Period: Closing will be conditioned on Buyer's approval, in Buyer's sole discretion, of title, inspection of the physical condition of the Property, Seller's documents related to the Property (including, among other things, all leases, rent rolls, service contracts, income operating history for *<year 1, year 2, year 3>*, and year to date (as available), surveys, building plans, permits, environmental and geo-technical reports, appraisals, and other documents in Seller's possession or control related to the Property), and Buyer's obtainment of financing. Buyer shall have up to *<sixty>* (60) days from delivery of Seller's documents to complete all due diligence (the "Contingency Period"). Seller will provide the documents and information to Buyer necessary to begin Buyer's due diligence within *<Five>* *(5)* days after Mutual Execution of the Purchase Agreement.

9. <u>Earnest Money:</u> Within *<Three>* *(3)* business days after Mutual Execution of the Purchase Agreement, Buyer shall deposit with the Escrow Company *<Earnest Money Amount>* (the "Earnest Money"). At closing, the Earnest Money and all interest shall be applied to the purchase price. If this transaction does not close and all conditions for the benefit of Buyer have been waived or satisfied, then the Earnest Money and all interest accruing thereon shall be paid to Seller, unless the transaction fails to close as a result of a condemnation, casualty, or default by Seller under the Purchase Agreement, in which case the Earnest Money shall be paid to Buyer. If Buyer timely terminates the transaction as a result of the failure of any condition, then the Earnest Money and any interest accruing will be paid to Buyer.

10. <u>Costs and Expenses:</u> At closing, Seller will pay for an ALTA standard policy of title insurance for the benefit of Buyer in the amount of the purchase price. Buyer shall pay for any additional title insurance coverage it elects to obtain. All closing costs and escrow fees will be shared equally between

Buyer and Seller. Property taxes, utilities, assessments, and all rents will be prorated as of the closing date. Seller shall pay all transfer taxes, and any deferred property taxes.

11. Assignment: Buyer may assign its rights under the Purchase Agreement in Buyer's sole discretion to an entity controlled by Buyer without Seller's consent. Any other assignment will require Seller's consent, which shall not be unreasonably withheld.

12. Personal Property: The Property will include all personal property, owned by Seller, located on the Property, and used in connection with the operation of the Property.

13. Commission: *<Choose either: List Commission being paid by seller or None>*.

14. Confidentiality: The parties agree to keep this transaction absolutely confidential and disclosure shall occur only as required by applicable law or as reasonably necessary in connection with the contemplated transaction.

15. Non-shop/Non-solicitation: Upon the execution of this Letter of Intent and until the transaction is closed or sooner terminated, neither Seller nor its agents shall seek or solicit any offers for the Property, nor shall they discuss or negotiate a possible sale of the Property with any person or entity other than with the Buyer.

If you find the above terms acceptable, please arrange to have a copy of this letter signed by the Seller and return it to me. Except for Paragraphs 14 and 15 above (Confidentiality and Non-Shop), which shall be binding on Buyer and Seller upon Mutual Execution of this Letter of Intent, neither party will be bound by any other term or provision of this Letter of Intent, unless or until a Purchase Agreement is signed by both parties.

This offer to purchase is valid for *<Five> (5)* business days after the date of this letter. By signing below, Buyer and Seller acknowledges receipt of a copy here of.

APPROVED AND ACCEPTED:

SELLER::

By:_____

Printed Name: _____

Title:_____

Date:_____

BUYER:

By: *<Name of LLC>*_____

Manager: _____

Printed Name: _____

*Date:*_____

The Purchase Contract

I prefer to use a custom contract wherever possible. It gives me more control over the transaction, and I can make sure that everything is included that needs to be. There are situations, however, where a boilerplate contract may be more palatable to a seller. If you use a LOI, it can make it easier for the seller to accept your contract.

There are a few steps that need to be followed in order to protect your interests:

- Always use an attorney to write the contract
- When dealing with partners, always use an escrow agent for all of the partnership money
- The contract should always have an effective date in addition to the date it was signed
- All of the contingencies can only be removed in writing
- Have all owner-paid utilities prorated
- All property taxes should be prorated

As a side point, it is important to prorate the property taxes based on the actual amount of taxes that are due, not just on the straight millage rate. Hold the amount for the taxes in an escrow account until the seller's share of the taxes are actually paid. I would recommend that you include a clause in the contract that states, "In the event the taxes are reduced, the savings are given to the buyer. In the event the taxes increase while the seller still holds title to the property, the proration shall be adjusted according to the new tax amount." When you become a seller, reverse the clause for your benefit.

Sample Contract Clauses

Before we break down the contract clauses, please understand that these clauses are geared to favor the buyer. You may not want to use all of them, or any of them, because the name of the game is to buy the property. Be willing to concede on some or all of these clauses, if you can get the property at a fair price and if it is necessary to facilitate the purchase.

The goal here with these clauses is to protect your money from "going hard" until you have performed all of your due diligence. If you can do that, this contract will keep you safe. When dealing with sellers directly, sometimes a short, simple contract is the best course of action. Again, just be sure you have a contingency to protect your money from going hard until you are certain you will be moving forward with the purchase. You do not want to lose your earnest money deposit under any circumstances. Some of these clauses will help ensure that does not happen.

Prorations

The Prorations shall be defined to mean prepaid rents, prepaid assessments, security deposits, prepaid or unpaid water and other utility or fuel charges, prepaid or unpaid service contracts, general or special real estate taxes or assessments, and other unpaid taxes. The Prorations shall be adjustments to the Purchase Price to reflect (a) credits to Purchaser for any liabilities or charges assumed, and (b) credits to Seller for amounts prepaid or otherwise credited for the benefit of Purchaser; provided, however, that the Prorations shall not include any adjustments for the benefit of Seller for any unpaid rents or assessments. The amount of any general real estate taxes not then ascertainable, if any, shall be adjusted on the basis of 105% of the most recent ascertainable general real estate taxes.

Purchaser's Rights Of Inspection And Cancellation

(a) Purchaser may inspect or cause to be inspected the condition of the Real Estate and all improvements and Personal Property;

(b) Purchaser may inspect or cause to be inspected all other documents and materials relating to the Real Estate and Personal Property;

(c) Within seven (7) days after the effective date of this agreement, Purchaser shall make a written request of Seller to deliver all documents and materials needed from Seller for inspection and evaluation. Upon receiving this written request from Purchaser, Seller shall deliver any such documents or materials requested within seven (7) days of Purchaser's request. Non-delivery of all requested information within 7 days shall be deemed Breach of Contract by Seller.

(d) After all documents and materials have been delivered to Purchaser, Purchaser may cancel this Agreement for any reason, at the sole discretion of Purchaser, within Forty-five (45) days after receiving all documents and materials from

Seller.

(e) In the event that Purchaser elects to cancel this Agreement during the initial 45-day inspection period, this paragraph shall serve as authority to the Escrow Agent from the Seller to act upon the "single order" of Purchaser to distribute the Earnest Money to Purchaser. Additionally, this paragraph shall serve as the Seller's release of the Escrow Agent from liability for disbursing the Earnest money to Purchaser.

(f) In the event any Third Party Reports are required by Purchaser or Purchaser's lender, and these Third Party Reports are not completed during this initial 45 day inspection period, the inspection period will automatically be extended for an additional ten (10) day period and Purchaser shall have the same rights of cancellation as Purchaser had during the initial 45 day inspection period.

(g) Seller shall allow Purchaser, or Purchaser's representatives, access or provide documents for review, whichever the case may be, of the Real Estate and Personal Property, at all reasonable times and shall cooperate with Purchaser's efforts to conduct the inspections permitted herein.

Title Insurance Survey And Environmental Study

(a) Title Insurance: Within _____ ( ) days from the date of this Agreement, Seller shall deliver a commitment for an ALTA owner's policy of title insurance that is reasonably acceptable to Purchaser (together with legible copies of all easements and restrictions of record identified by the commitment), in the full amount of the purchase price, evidencing Seller's good and merchantable title to the Real Estate. If title to all or part of the Property is unmarketable, as determined by relevant law, or is subject to liens, encumbrances, easements, conditions, restrictions or encroachments other than those disclosed in this Agreement, Buyer or Buyer's attorney shall give written notice of such defect to Seller within a reasonable time. Seller agrees to make every reasonable effort to perfect the title including the issuance of a title affidavit. Seller shall have a reasonable time to have such title defects removed or such defects or exceptions, which may be removed by the payment of money, may be cured by deduction from the purchase price at the time of closing. If Seller is unable to cure title, then Buyer shall have the option to

terminate this Agreement, in which case Buyer shall be entitled to a refund of the earnest money. If closing is delayed due to Seller's inability to provide marketable title, this Agreement shall continue in force and effect until either party rescinds this Agreement until making a reasonable effort to produce marketable title in the prescribed time. Furnishing a title insurance policy insuring over an exception shall constitute a cure of such exception in those cases where title is evidenced by title insurance. The Title Insurance policy shall be paid for by Seller at closing.

(b) Survey: Within Thirty (30) days from the date of this Agreement, Seller shall deliver to Purchaser a copy of the existing Survey of the Real Estate. If an existing Survey is not available, then Seller shall obtain a new Boundary Survey at Purchaser's cost.

(c) Environmental study: Purchaser may obtain, at Purchaser's expense, an environmental study of the Real Estate. Purchaser shall be responsible for the cost of the environmental study.

The Closing

Subject to Purchaser's right to terminate this Agreement, as set forth in Paragraph 3 (c) above, the closing of this transaction shall be held no later than 15 days after the Purchaser's right of inspection and cancellation period expires, as described in Paragraph_____, above, unless earlier extended in writing and signed by mutual agreement of the Seller and the Purchaser. The closing shall take place at the title company serving as escrow agent for the earnest deposit. The time of the closing shall be a mutually convenient time for the Purchaser and Seller.

Purchaser's Closing Instruments

At closing, Purchaser shall deliver to Seller the following instruments:

(a) A cashier's check, or wire transfer, for the amount required by Paragraph _____ .

(b) Any other instruments reasonably necessary to complete the transaction contemplated hereby.

Seller' Closing Instruments

At the closing, Seller shall deliver to Purchaser the following documents:

(a) Warranty Deed reasonably acceptable to Purchaser conveying good title in the Real Estate, as described herein, and a transfer of title agreement reasonably acceptable to Purchaser conveying good title in the Personal Property as described herein;

(b) Any other instruments reasonably necessary to complete the transaction herein.

Possession

Purchaser shall take possession of all of the Real Estate and Personal Property at closing.

Proations, Transfer Taxes And Closing Costs

Prorations shall take place at the time of closing. All deposits shall be transferred to Purchaser at closing, including but not limited to security deposits from residents and advanced rental deposits from residents. Purchaser and Seller shall pay their usual and customary portion of transfer taxes at the time of closing. All remaining closing costs, which have not been addressed by this Agreement, shall be shared equally by Purchaser and Seller.

Cross Indemnification

Seller hereby agrees to indemnify Purchaser and hold and save Purchaser harmless from and against all liabilities, debts, claims, actions, causes of action, losses, damages and attorney's fees, now existing or that may hereafter arise from or grow out of Seller's past ownership of the Real Estate and Personal Property, that are of the subject of this Agreement, and which occurred through the date of closing. Purchaser hereby agrees to indemnify Seller and hold and save Seller harmless from and against all liabilities, debts, claims, actions, or causes of action, losses, damages and attorney's fees, that may arise from or grow out of Purchaser's ownership of the Real Estate and Personal Property, that are the subject of this Agreement after the date of closing.

Seller and Purchaser acknowledge that this contemplated transaction includes only the sale and purchase of the Real Estate and Personal Property, and that the Seller is not selling a business, nor do the parties intend that Purchaser be deemed a successor of Seller with respect to any liabilities of Seller to any third parties.

Accordingly, Purchaser shall neither assume nor be liable for any payments or benefits to past and/or present employees of Seller in connection with the Business being conducted on or from the Property as may have accrued through the Closing Date, including, but not limited to, salaries, wages, commission, bonuses, vacation pay, health and welfare contributions, pensions, profit sharing, severance or termination pay, taxes, or any other form of compensation or fringe benefit. The representations and indemnities set forth in this section shall survive the Closing or the earlier termination of this contract.

Commissions Due

Six percent (6%) of the purchase price shall be payable to XYZ Realty from the Seller's proceeds.

Or: There are no real estate commissions due for this transaction.

Purchaser's Representations And Warranties

Purchaser hereby represents and warrants to Seller as follows:

(a) Purchaser warrants that it is a Limited Liability Company duly organized, validly existing, and in good standing under the laws of the State of _____ ;

(b) Purchaser warrants that it has full power and authority to execute, deliver, and perform this Agreement;

(c) Purchaser warrants that the execution, delivery, and performance of this Agreement by Purchaser have been duly authorized by all requisite actions on the part of Purchaser;

(d) Purchaser warrants that it has no judgment against it in any court of law or equity, nor does Purchaser have knowledge of any claims that may lead to the institution of legal proceedings against it;

(e) Purchaser warrants that all representations and warranties of Purchaser in this Agreement are true, accurate, and complete in all material respects as of the date hereof, and will be true, accurate and complete in all material respects as of the date of closing.

All representations and warranties of Purchaser contained in this Agreement, and all remedial provisions contained herein, shall be deemed remade at closing and shall survive the closing.

Seller's Representations And Warranties

Seller hereby represents and warrants to Purchaser as follows:

(a) Seller warrants that there are no claims, actions, suits, or proceedings pending or threatened on account of or as a result of Seller's ownership of the Real Estate and Personal Property, which, if adversely determined, would have an adverse impact on the value of the Real Estate and Personal Property, or would prevent or hinder the consummation of the transaction contemplated herein;

(b) Seller warrants that Seller has good and merchantable title in fee simple to the Real Estate and Personal Property that are subject to this Agreement, and the Seller has not entered into any leases,licenses,options,easements or other agreements, recorded or unrecorded, granting rights to any parties in any of the assets, other than to renters in the apartment community, and no person or other entity has any right to possession or occupancy of any of the assets, other than renters in the community;

(c) Seller warrants that there exists no violation of any Federal, State, County, or any other laws or ordinances, with respect to the occupancy, use, and operation of the Real Estate.

(d) Seller warrants that Seller is not in default under or in violation of any contract, commitment, or restriction to which they are a party or by which they are bound, which default or violation would have a material and adverse effect on this transaction;

144

(e) Seller warrants that they are not aware that there has ever been or is currently any hazardous substances, generated, stored, buried, placed, held, located or disposed of on, under or at the Real Estate and the Real Estate has never been used as a dump site, and there are no, nor have there ever been any, underground storage tanks in or on the Real Estate.

The definition of "Hazardous substances" shall mean all hazardous or toxic materials, substances, pollutants, contaminants or wastes currently identified as a hazardous substance or waste in the Comprehensive Environmental Response, Compensation and Liability Act of 1980 (commonly known as "CERCLA"), as amended, the Super fund Amendments and Preauthorization Act (commonly known as "SARA"), as amended, the Resource Conservation and Recovery Act (commonly known as "RCRA"), as amended, or any other federal, state or local legislation or ordinances applicable to the Real Estate or Personal Property;

(f) Seller warrants that to the best of Seller's knowledge all power supplies/systems owned by Seller meet the current code requirements, as well as any change mandates that are in effect. Additionally, Seller warrants that to the best of Seller's knowledge, there are no existing or pending regulatory requirements that must be satisfied for Seller to complete this Agreement with Purchaser. Additionally, Seller warrants that to the best of Seller's knowledge, there is no other study, report, or finding which indicates that any portion of the Real Estate is located in a floodplain or is unsuitable for building purposes;

(g) Seller warrants that to the best of Seller's knowledge the water and sewer systems, together with all mechanical systems serving the subject Real Estate and Personal Property, are in sound operating condition, free from hidden or latent defects, and are adequate in size and performance to properly serve the needs of the existing community in its entire developed capacity. At Closing, Seller shall deliver, and convey all architectural, structural, physical, and infrastructure plans, drawings, specifications, and renderings related to the Real Estate in his possession. Additionally, Seller shall deliver and convey original copies of all appropriate tenant files, including signed rules and leases; and   .

(h) Seller warrants that to the best of Seller's knowledge, all representations and warranties of Seller in this Agreement are

true, accurate, and complete in all material respects as of the date hereof, and will be true, accurate, and complete in all material respects as of the date of closing.

(i) Seller has no actual knowledge of (1) notice of city, county, state, federal, building, zoning, fire or health codes, regulations or ordinances filed or contemplated against the Property, (2) current pending lawsuit(s), investigation(s) inquiry(ies), action(s), or other proceeding(s) affecting the right to use and occupy the Property, (3) unsatisfied construction liens, (4) tenants in bankruptcy, or (5) pending or threatened condemnation, eminent domain, changes in grade of public streets affecting the Property or similar proceedings affecting the Property or (6) of any unfulfilled order or directive of any applicable governmental agency or casualty insurance company requiring any investigation, remediation, repair, maintenance or improvement be performed on the Property. If Seller has any knowledge regarding the above mentioned items, Seller shall provide a listing and description of actions.

(j) Seller shall maintain the Property, including landscaping and grounds, in its present condition, ordinary wear and tear excepted. Purchaser shall be permitted to make a final inspection prior to possession or closing, whichever is sooner, in order to determine that there has been no change in the condition of the property.

(k) Seller agrees to provide Purchaser full disclosure of any and all free, discounted or prepaid rents, rents paid in forms other than cash, and lease agreements other than the disclosed tenant leases, that may be in effect currently or beyond the scheduled Closing Date. Seller warrants that unless otherwise indicated by the rent roll provided, no other tenants are in default or arrears. Seller hereby covenants not to terminate any existing lease or occupancy agreement or enter into any new leases or occupancy agreements without obtaining Purchaser's consent thereto. Nothing contained herein shall limit the right of Seller to continue to enforce individual leases in ordinary course of business or to operate the Real Estate up to Closing.

(l) Seller warrants that it has full power and authority to execute, deliver and perform this Agreement, no other third-party approvals are required, and that performance of this agreement will not violate any other agreements to which the Seller is a party.

(m) Seller warrants that to the best of Seller's knowledge all representations and warranties of Seller in this Agreement are true, accurate, and complete in all material respects as of the date hereof, and will be true, accurate and complete in all material respects as of the date of Closing.

Inspection Contingency

The Buyer may, at the Buyer's own expense and within ten (10) days from the date of the acceptance of this Offer, have the property professionally inspected for any or all of the following:

1. *Property Inspection (structural, electrical, mechanical, general condition)*
2. *Termite, Wood-Boring Insects, Pest Inspection*
3. *On-Site Sewer Disposal Inspection*
4. *Lead Paint Inspection*
5. *Radon Gas Inspection*
6. *Asbestos Inspection*
7. *Urea Formaldehyde Foam Insulation (UFFI) Inspection*
8. *Chlordane Inspection*
9. *Hazardous Materials, Groundwater and Soil Test Inspection (may require longer than 10 days to successfully complete)*
10. *Well Test Inspection (water quality and quantity)*
11. *Other*

Should any of the above-listed inspections reveal the existence of unsatisfactory or hazardous conditions with the property, then the Buyer shall send written notice of same to the Broker and Seller on or before by certified mail, return receipt requested, facsimile, or by hand delivery to the Seller and the Broker with a copy of the inspection findings to be provided to the Seller and the Broker within seven (7) days following notification. Upon receipt of the written notification and a copy of the inspection findings by the Seller, this Offer/Purchase and Sale Agreement shall become NULL AND VOID immediately, and upon the issuance of mutually agreeable instructions by Buyer(s) and Seller(s) and upon the signing of a Release by all parties, then all deposits made hereunder shall forthwith be refunded to the Buyer, and all parties to this Offer/ Purchase and Sale Agreement shall be released from allliability.

147

Mortgage Contingency

In order to help finance the acquisition of said premises, the Buyer shall apply for a conventional bank or other institutional mortgage loan of $_____ at prevailing rates, terms and conditions. If, despite the Buyer's diligent efforts, a commitment for such a loan cannot be obtained on or before_____, the Buyer may terminate this agreement by written notice to the Seller and/or the Broker(s), as agent(s) for the Seller, prior to the expiration of such time, whereupon any payments made under this agreement shall be forthwith refunded and all other obligation of the parties hereto shall cease and this agreement shall be void without recourse to the parties hereto. In no event will the Buyer be deemed to have used diligent efforts to obtain such commitment unless the Buyer submits a complete mortgage loan application conforming to the foregoing provisions on or before_____.

General Terms

Seller shall bear the risk of loss or damage to the property prior to possession or closing, whichever first occurs. In the event of substantial damage or destruction prior to closing, this Agreement shall be null and void, unless otherwise agreed by the Parties. The property shall be deemed substantially damaged or destroyed if it cannot be restored to its present condition on or before the closing date, provided, however, Purchaser shall have the right to complete the closing and receive insurance proceeds regardless of the extent of the damages.

Special assessments levied or to be levied for improvements completed, or where NOTICE of RESOLUTION for improvements is in effect previous to the Effective Date but not yet levied, shall be paid by Seller. An assessment which cannot be determined or discharged by payments shall be escrowed with sufficient funds to pay such liens when payable. Excess funds are to be returned to the Seller without further signature of Buyer.

Escrow Fund Instructions

All deposits made hereunder shall be held in Escrow by_____: as Escrow agent, in their non-interest bearing account, subject to the terms of this agreement and shall be duly accounted for at the time for performance of this agreement. In the event of any disagreement between the parties, the Escrow agent may retain all deposits made under this agreement, pending instructions mutually given by the Seller and Buyer.

Broker No Representation Or Warranties

The Broker(s) named herein, and their agents, make no representations, guarantees, or warranties (express or implied) concerning the condition of the premises, or the boundaries of said premises except as herein stated; notwithstanding any other terms of the agreement, this paragraph will survive delivery of this agreement.

Notices

All notices that may be required by this Agreement shall be sent to the respective parties at the addresses appearing below:

"Purchaser"   *"Seller"*

_____   _____

Purchaser's LLC name   *Seller's name*

Purchaser's LLC address   *Seller's address*

PH: _____   *P   H   :*

_____

FX: _____   *F   X   :*

_____

Any such notices shall be (i) personally delivered to the office set forth above, in which case they shall be deemed delivered on the date of delivery to said offices, (ii) sent by certified mail, return receipt requested, in which case they shall be deemed delivered three (3) days after deposit in the U.S. mail, postage prepaid, (iii) sent by facsimile, in which case they shall be deemed delivered on the date of transmission (if before 5:00 p.m. CST), (iv) sent by air courier (Federal Express or like service), in which case they shall be deemed delivered on the date of actual delivery or (v) sent via email with confirmation from the receiving party that such email was received. Either party may change the address to which any such notice is to be delivered by furnishing written notice of such change to the other party via one of the above methods in compliance with the foregoing provisions.

Arbitration

In the event that a dispute arises over the terms of this Agreement, the parties agree to submit to binding arbitration to resolve such dispute. The arbitration shall be conducted in accordance with the Expedited Procedures of the Commercial Arbitration Rules of the American Arbitration Association at a hearing to be held in or near the City in which the property is located and the laws of the state in which the property is located shall govern. Any decision reached from such arbitration shall have the same binding authority as if it were decided by a court of competent jurisdiction. The more prevailing party shall be entitled to the reimbursement of all costs, including reasonable attorney's fees from the other party.

Default

In the event the transaction contemplated hereby does not close or is terminated due to a default by Seller, Purchaser shall be entitled to immediate return of the Earnest Money and may pursue all its rights and remedies at law and in equity, including, without limitation, specific performance. In the event the transaction contemplated hereby does not close or is terminated due to a default by Purchaser in the performance of its obligations under the Agreement, Seller, as their sole remedy, either at law or in equity, shall be entitled to retain the Earnest Money as liquidated damages.

In the event of a default by either party hereto, the party not in default shall give notice thereof to the defaulting party and an opportunity to cure for a period of five (5) days following the delivery of notice, prior to exercising any right or remedy to which the party not in default may be entitled.

Entire Agreement

This Agreement constitutes the entire agreement between the parties pertaining to the subject matter contained herein and supersedes all prior and contemporaneous agreements or representations whether written or oral. This Agreement may only be modified if the modification is made in writing and signed by both Purchaser and Seller. No oral modifications shall be permitted. This Agreement is binding upon, and inures to the benefit of, the parties hereto and their heirs, executors, administrators, successors and assigns.

Definition Of Time

For purposes of this Agreement, the term "Day" shall mean calendar day, unless otherwise specified. The time in which any act provided by this Agreement is to be done shall be computed by excluding the first day and including the last, unless the last day is a Saturday, Sunday or Holiday, in which case it also shall be excluded. If any deadline set forth herein falls on a Saturday, Sunday or Holiday, the deadline shall be extended to the next business day.

Subject To All Applicable Laws

This Agreement is intended to be performed in accordance with, and only to the extent permitted by, all applicable laws, ordinances, rules, and circumstances. If, for any reason, and to any extent, any portion of this Agreement shall be held to be invalid or unenforceable, the remainder of this Agreement shall be enforced as if such invalid or unenforceable provision did not exist, and such valid and enforceable remainder shall be enforced to the greatest extent as permitted by law.

Time Is Of The Essence

Time is of the essence of this Agreement, and of each provision thereof.

Acceptance

This offer shall expire and become null and void if not accepted by Seller and delivered to Purchaser within_____ (__) days of the date of this Agreement.

Legal Counsel Acknowledgment

Buyer and Seller acknowledge that they have each been advised of the importance of seeking legal advice prior to signing the Purchase and Sale Agreement, and each acknowledges that they have been afforded the opportunity to confer with legal counsel of their choice prior to signing the Purchase and Sale Agreement.

Chapter 18
Killer Due Diligence

Careful and comprehensive due diligence is one of the most important aspects of multifamily real estate investing. It is important that you familiarize yourself with it. If you cut corners or ignore the due diligence process, you can leave tens to hundreds of thousands of dollars on the table. Even worse, you could make the huge mistake of moving forward on a deal that you wouldn't have, had you completed the due diligence more carefully.

It is very common for investors to back out of a deal based on what they have found during their due diligence search. It is much wiser to spend whatever it takes on your due diligence, only to find out it is a bad deal and back out, than it is to close your eyes to potential problems and regret it later. Smart investors know sometimes the best deals are the ones they don't buy.

Purchasing commercial investment property is very different than simply buying a residential home. When you are buying a house, you have a lot of consumer protection laws that can protect you in that transaction. Those laws do not apply in commercial real estate transactions. Even though the purchase agreement will include representations and warranties, they in no way replace comprehensive due diligence.

Consumer protection laws do not apply in commercial real estate transactions.

The Resources

Before you begin the inspection phase of the due diligence period, you should have collected information about the property and the neighborhood. You will use this information to answer quite a few questions about the property.

What You Need From The Seller

At some point in the transaction, either around the time of the Letter of Intent or more likely after the signing of the actual sales contract, you will need to make a request of the seller for all of the property's financial, leasing, operational and legal paperwork. Keep a copy for your records, because you will find yourself going back to it before the due diligence is completed. You will need to get copies of as much of the following as you possibly can:

Financials

- Last 2 years of financial operating statements
- A year-to-date operating statement
- Last 6 months of bank statements (used to match against the rent roll and operating statements)
- Utility deposit register
- Utility bills for the last two years
- Property tax bills for the last two years
- IRS Tax returns and addenda for the last two years (as related to the property only)

Tenant Information

- Rent roll for the property for the last two years
- Security deposit register
- Payroll records
- Each different lease type
- Written property policies, such as for pets and parking
- Information on all rent concessions

Management Information

- Commission agreements with the leasing staff
- Current property management contract
- List of any uncompleted maintenance requests
- Maintenance and capital improvement history for past three years (look for common recurring problems)
- Litigation history on the property for the past five years

Property Information

- Service contracts including pool, trash, laundry, extermination, snow plowing, elevator service,etc.
- HVAC and/or boiler reports
- Elevator maintenance report
- Insurance policy
- Insurance claims history for the past two years
- Any operation manuals for the property
- Business license
- Deed

- Title policy
- Property survey
- Site plan
- Architectural plans
- Environmental Reports
- Any mold inspection reports
- Any lead-based paint inspection reports
- Any fire system reports or citations
- Inventory of property tools, supplies and personal property

What you Need From Others

- *Demographic and Crime Reports for the area.* We listed websites previously like www.spotcrime.com for this purpose.

- *A market survey of comparable properties.* This would include not only comparable listings but also existing competitive properties. Call the competition around the subject property and mystery shop them. You can also ask brokers in the area.

- *Contact the local Chamber of Commerce.* I think it is always a good idea to find out what is happening in the area.
    - Are there any financial incentives for investing in the area?
    - What new businesses are coming to the area?
    - Is the market population expanding or contracting? Why?

- *Speak to the City or County Planning and Zoning Offices.* Your goal here is to find out what is the history with the subject property.
    - Does the property density conform to current zoning?
    - Have there been any code violations in the last 3 years?
    - Have any permits been pulled on the property for any reason whatsoever in the last 5 years?
    - Is the building ADA compliant?

- *Meet with the County or City Assessor.* Ask them what they know about the property and the market area.
    - Are assessed values increasing and if so, by what annual percentage?
    - Are there any concessions attached to this property?
    - Have the property owners contested the property taxes within the past 3 years? If so, what was the outcome?

- *Call the plumbers, electricians, HVAC contractors, maintenance men, and general contractors who have worked on the property.* I like to talk to them and get their opinion on the property. I will ask them these questions:
  - What do you think about the infrastructure?
  - What problems have you encountered?
  - Are you aware of any deferred maintenance issues?
  - Are there any common area improvements that are needed?
  - The building systems are in what kind of condition?
  - What is your opinion of the roof, plumbing, mechanical, and electrical systems? Does anything need replacing, repairing or an upgrade?
  - Are the buildings up to current code?
  - Are you willing to come and inspect the property? Using a contractor already familiar with the property can be useful.
  - I also regularly contact vendors that never worked on the property to get assessments of conditions. Sometimes tenured vendors for that property will mitigate their own deficiencies by not fully disclosing everything wrong with the property.
- *Meet with your lender.*
  - If you find areas of deferred maintenance, it is important to include them in your budget analysis and underwriting.
  - At some point in your due diligence, you will need to confirm that the debt coverage ratio is acceptable to your lender.
  - Will the lender require any hold backs of your funds or require you to hold reserves for future capital expenditures?

What Can You Collect Yourself?

- *Pictures and videos of the property.* Do not trust your memory. You will have a lot of things on your mind. Do not take the chance that you will forget the missing shingles or the water damage in one of the apartments. Just snap a picture or a quick video and analyze it later.

- *Aerial pictures of the property.* Getting a bird's eye view can help to identify encroachments. It also will help you to get the big picture of the neighborhood. Aerial pictures can be found on <u>Google Earth</u> and often are part of the County records. We have a drone that we use.

- *Measure tenant demand.* An easy way to measure the demand for these rental units is to run an ad for one of the units on <u>Craigslist</u>. The response will help you to see how easy it will be to rent out those units. A high volume of response can indicate that the rental rate is too low.

The Basics

When you start your due diligence, you need some facts about the property and neighborhood. While some of these questions may have been answered during the preliminary pre-due diligence phase, now is the time to dig a little deeper.

The Neighborhood

- What are the crime statistics for the area?
- Who are the major employers in the area?
- What sort of retail stores are nearby?
- Where is the closest grocery and pharmacy?
- How far are schools and parks from the property?
- How far away are the police and fire stations?
- What is the vacancy in the area for similar types of properties?
- Is there nearby access to public transportation?

The Physical Property

- What is the physical age of the property?
- What is the condition of the property?
- Is there adequate parking?
- Is there guest parking?
- What are the options for laundry for the tenants?
- Does the property have amenities like a pool or a club house?
- Are there any easements on the property?
- Are there any covenants that stay with the land?
- Are there any encroachments on the property?
- Is the building ADA compliant?

The Property Management

- What is the tenant mix in the property?
- How many one, two, and three bedroom units are in the property?
- What is the vacancy of the property over the past 3 years?
- Is the overall occupancy dropping or improving? How does it compare to the competition?
- Is the current management offering concessions to get people in the property?
- Is the management offering any capital improvements or concessions on lease renewals?
- Are any of the utilities included in the rent?
- How many leases will expire within the next 90 days?
- When was the last time rents were raised and by how much?

When you are evaluating the income and expenses, make sure you look at every line on those reports.

- The Income
  - Has the income been consistent every month?
  - Are there any anomalies that you need to investigate further?
  - Does the P&L match the bank statements or tax returns?
- The Expenses: A careful analysis of the expenses will cause you to see any anomalies. It is not uncommon for sellers to leave expenses off of the financial statements to make the property look more attractive. Remember, though, that every property is unique and may have specific expenses relating to that region or area that need to be considered.
  - Do the maintenance expenses look realistic or are they low? Typically, they should amount to at least 5 to 10% of the gross income.
  - How does the expense ratio compare to other multi- family properties in the area? A total of a 50% expense ratio is common for many multifamily properties.
  - Are the expenses on this property higher? If so, in what categories? If they are lower, are there capital expenditures or maintenance items that have been missed?
  - How consistent have the expenses been over the past 3years?
  - Are the operating expenses, which were disclosed in the seller's documents, the same as the operating expenses in the listing information and tax records?

- The Net Operating Income
  - What is the current NOI?
  - How is it trending? It is important to look at the last 12 months to see if it is increasing or dropping, make sure you find out why.
  - What percentage of the gross income does the NOI represent? Typically the NOI is 50% of the gross annual income.

It is critical to make sure you plug in adequate reserves into your underwriting for any immediate and future repairs or capital expenditures.

The Tenants

- Visit the property at night

  - What is the age and condition of the vehicles?
  - Do you feel safe?
  - What is your gut feeling?

- Talk to some of the tenants.

  - How do they like living there?
  - How is the building maintained?
  - What changes would you like to see happen?
  - When your lease expires, do you think you will stay or move?
  - Would you say that this is a quiet or loud building?

A second or third opinion never hurts. I find that it is always a great idea to talk to other real estate brokers about the area that you are interested in and even that specific property. You may be surprised by how much they know about it. This is a very valuable way to mitigate risk and help prevent mistakes during the due diligence process.

The Inspection

The physical property inspection is a crucial part of the due diligence process. While you most likely visited the property before submitting an offer, this inspection must be done carefully and with a critical eye.

You are no longer simply looking at the property to see if it would meet your business or investment needs. This inspection is primarily focused on the physical condition of the property and any risks (both physical and financial) that are presently on site.

During the physical inspection, it is important to take excellent and detailed notes. Do not rush. I would recommend you video record as much as possible. To make sure you do not miss anything while recording, it may be a good idea to bring along an assistant to run the camera while you do the actual inspection.

The human eye can only focus on one thing at a time. This can make it very easy to miss something. In order to accurately complete a physical inspection, you may want to make several visits to the property. I would even recommend that you go by the property on different days of the week and at different times of the day. This will help you assess the quality of tenants and the general atmosphere surrounding the property. Even if this is not your first investment property purchase, do not be afraid to bring in some professional help. This may include structural engineers, commercial HVAC companies, plumbers, electricians, exterminators, and the like. Ask for written reports after the inspection. Paying for their services could save you thousands of dollars.

When you go through the inspection, make sure you inspect each and every unit. The seller, or their agent, may just open the *State in the contract that the due diligence period must be waived in writing.* door to every second or third unit. Which unit do you think the seller or their manager will voluntarily show you – the recently remodeled one or the apartment that has issues? It is a painfully long process, but before you spend hundreds of thousands of dollars, you need to know exactly what you are buying and the condition of each unit. Do not trust that the seller, or their broker, will disclose the true condition of the property. You may have read "Recently renovated and updated" on the listing sheet, but they never told you it was 2 units out of 65. Put forth the effort and take the time to inspect every unit.

The Re-Trade Or Negotiation

Depending on what you find through your due diligence process, you may feel that your initial purchase price was too high, particularly if what the seller represented was not what you found. Maybe you found other issues, problems or factors that could impact your offer price.

Either way, you as the buyer have the right to re-negotiate with the seller for a price reduction. Obviously, the seller is not required to accept your new price. They have the right to insist on the original price and/or a cancellation of the contract, which would mean a return of your earnest money deposit.

When it comes to discussing a reduced purchase price with the seller, be sure to have all of your documentation in hand. It's important to ask yourself some questions. What is the seller's motivation for selling? Does he need a rapid sale? How badly do you want to purchase this property?

Work towards a win-win situation. Work to make it so the seller will not walk away from the table feeling like their property has been stolen from them. Remember to get something for everything you concede.

The Walk-Away Price

Before you sit down with the seller, you need to know your "walk-away" price. Based on the information that was revealed in the due diligence, what is the most that you would be willing to spend?

Remember to take into consideration your lender's requirements. The debt-to-income ratio must work. The loan-to-value must also meet the lender's requirements. Before you set the "walk-away" price, factor in the likelihood of being able to get funding for the purchase.

Be Prepared

The seller is expecting to close on the original purchase price. They're not going to want to lower it. They're already dreaming about spending the profits. If you want to negotiate a better deal, you're going to have to be prepared.

You are going to need to come to the negotiating table with facts and figures to back up your claim. It may be several estimates on how much it will cost to replace the leaking roof. It may be an adjusted Profit and Loss Statement based on the actual numbers. Whatever proof you have, bring it with you. Showing evidence that backs up your request for a price reduction is critical to a successful negotiation.

Do not expect to have all of your demands met. This can work to your advantage. Prepare a list that includes critical "must haves" and "would like" items. Then, as the negotiations progress, you can back off some of your lesser items. The seller will feel better about the transaction, and you will get what you absolutely need to make the deal happen. Focus on win-win, because the seller will feel your energy.

It is a good idea to practice your pitch. Your confidence level can go a long way to prove to the seller that you are not low balling, and you seriously believe the market value is lower.

Meet The Deadline

As you know, purchase contracts alway shave due diligence deadlines. We recommend the contract clearly states the due diligence is not waived unless done so in writing by a certain date. If you feel the need to negotiate a price reduction, make sure it is handled within the due diligence period. If you believe this cannot happen before the due diligence period expires, pursue an extension or cancel the contract.

Sitting At The Table

Renegotiations can get tense. Keep your emotions in check. Calmly and professionally explain why you see the need to offer a reduced price or to add certain contingencies. Re-read the negotiation strategies previously in this book.

Again, be willing to give and take. Remember your "walk-away" price and stick to it. Once an agreement has been made, get it in writing. Get it in writing right then and there – even if you have to scratch it out on a yellow pad of paper. You can get it typed up when you get back into the office. Writing it out then and there will make sure nothing is missed and that both the seller and the buyer understand the summary of the negotiation.

Once you get back to the office, have your broker, or preferably your attorney, draft the addendum to the purchase agreement, and then have all the parties sign it. Until it is signed and dated by all parties, it is not binding. You can then progress to the closing. Make sure you send a copy of the addendum or new contract to your lender so that they can adjust their documents and use the new purchase price in all their paperwork and closing documents.

Chapter 19
Property Management

How you manage your property can make or break your success. You could find a highly discounted and newly remodeled apartment building that is running at 100% occupancy and run it into the ground in a few years with poor management. Knowing how to effectively monitor and manage your real estate investments is a skill that is absolutely imperative to master.

There are two schools of thought from successful real estate investors. Many, like myself, believe you should self-manage, while others believe you should always hire a management company. It is my opinion, whether you do it yourself or you utilize a management company, you have to fully understand the property management business. Even if you hire a property management company, you will still need to manage them. You will still need to make crucial management decisions. That is why you need to understand all of the nuances of managing multifamily real estate.

The primary reason I advocate managing your own properties, at least initially, is because understanding the management process is so important. If and when you decide to hire a property management company, you will fully understand the business and can monitor and manage them to make a success of your investment.

At one point in my real estate career, I owned over 200 houses in the Memphis, Tennessee area. I had hired a local property manager to look after these investments since I was not living near there. Because I wasn't keeping my eye on the ball and I was relying too heavily on the property manager, she was able to embezzle over $100,000 from me. The property manager was claiming the area suffered from high vacancy, which was why so many of my units were vacant. In actuality, she had rented them out and was collecting the rents directly in cash. It didn't take many houses and or very many months for the money to quickly add up. If I had been more on top of things and paid more attention to my investments and my property manager, this would never have happened.

Taking Over Management

There are a lot of details to look after as you take over the management of an apartment complex.

- *Notify the current residents of the change in management.* Prepare a letter for each of the residents. You can mail it or slide it under their door. The letter will explain how they will do business with the new management moving forward. It should include items such as:
  - Name, address and phone number of the new owner
  - Name, address and phone number of the property management company (if applicable)
  - How the rent can be paid – online, bank draft, check, etc.
  - Where to mail the rent
  - Who and how to contact for maintenance and other issues
  - Who to contact in case of emergency
- *Update tenant information.* When you send the letter to the residents, use this time to update/double check tenant contact information. Simply include a form they can fill out, a link to your website, or an email address where they can fill in the following information:
  - Names, age, and relationship of all residents
  - Contact information
  - Current employer information, including phone number, in case of an emergency
- *Notify utility companies.* Contact the utility companies and file a change of ownership/address.
- *Contact the local fire and police departments.* Provide them with your contact information and the contact information of your property manager, if applicable, in case there is an emergency at the property.
- *Contact all current vendors.* You should update/rewrite all contracts. This would include the contractors that provide the following services:
  - Swimming Pool Maintenance
  - Parking Lot Maintenance
  - Landscapers/Lawn Maintenance
  - HVAC
  - Plumbers
  - Electricians
  - Pest Control
  - Vending Machine Servicing
  - Washer/Dryer Equipment Owners

I would recommend you also set up a purchase order "PO" system and require your vendors to work from a PO. Remind them if they do work without a PO, they may not get paid. You should also negotiate a payment/check cycle. I would recommend at least 30-day payment terms.

- *Set up a property-specific checking account.* Make sure the account is in the name of the entity listed on the title. That account will be for the NOI from the property. Your personal or hired property management company will deposit rents and pay expenses for the property, and they will send the NOI to you. Keep the income and expenses for your real estate completely separate from your personal finances.

- *Set up an accounting system.* Work with your accountant to set up an initial chart of accounts.

  - Many investors make the common mistake of misclassifying expenses. If you want to make sure you do not pay too much in taxes, learn what the difference is between an expense and a capital improvement. It will impact your taxes and the value of your property when it comes time to sell or refinance.

  - Decide if you will utilize cash or accrual method of accounting.

  - Determine the depreciation schedule for your assets. Be sure to explore "cost segregation."

- *Create management systems.* If you are planning on managing the investment yourself, you are going to need to setup systems and procedures for numerous aspects of the management. It is critical to create these systems in writing. Not only will it keep the management consistent, but it will also be essential when you bring in other people on your team or hand over the management to a professional company. You should set up systems for:

  - Rent collections
  - Late pay procedures
  - Maintenance systems and procedures
  - Lease up procedures
  - Accounting procedures
  - Property upkeep and scheduled maintenance
  - Marketing systems
  - Purchase Order system

The property management business is very form and checklist intensive. You will need to ensure all of your forms, checklists, and documentation are ready as soon as possible after you start the management. Taking the time to frame out your ownership and management policies will go a long way to reducing stress and creating a consistent cash flow down the road. Please do not skip this step. It may be a hassle, but it is completely worth the effort.

Property Management Software

When you start managing your own property, you are going to need some good property management software. Don't take shortcuts. You may be tempted to just set up an Excel file, but good software can make your life much easier. Even Quickbooks is better than just using a spreadsheet.

I have used Yardi for years, and I love it. There are lots of different software companies that offer a variety of products. Here are some of my recommendations:

- Yardi (www.yardi.com). (Variable Cost) A great software package that streamlines marketing, leasing, tenant screening, rent collection, and accounting. It allows tenants to pay online and submit maintenance requests.
- Rent Manager (www.rentmanager.com).($75/month minimum) An all-in-one software package that can handle any size portfolio, integrating accounting, VoIP, online tenant portals, screening, and electronic payments.

Never shortcut the application & screening process.

- Buildium (learn.buildium.com). (Starts at $150/month) This is a full-featured, web-based software solution that focuses on residential and association properties. Tenants can submit requests online, which can be converted into a work order. Works with QuickBooks.
- Flex (www.flexrentalsolutions.com).($270 a month w/ a one- time $800 setup fee). A web-based customizable package that manages tenants but does not offer accounting. Can be linked to QuickBooks.
- LandlordMax (www.landlordmax.com). ($199 1 User/Unlimited Units). Quick setup, no monthly or annual fees. Offers detailed reporting and cross- referencing. Users say it is easy to use.

- Appfolio (www.appfolio.com).($250/month minimum). A cloud based software system that accepts and sends out electronic payments, offers easy vacancy posting, website hosting, online maintenance requests, applications and lease signing and even in-app texting.
- TrueRent (www.truerent.com). ($1 per unit/per month with a $15/month minimum.) Rent collection, tenant screening, accounting, document management, and a tenant portal. It even integrates alerts and reminders for rents due, lease expirations, etc.

Know The Law

More than simply collecting the rent and fixing a dripping faucet, it is critical to review and fully understand the Landlord-Tenant laws where your property is located. Some areas have unusual or even landlord-adverse/tenant-friendly laws. What is more, tenants know how to find this stuff online and use it against you. I have heard numerous war stories from inexperienced landlords who did not realize there were rent controls in place before they bought the property.

Remember that Memphis, Tennessee market? I experienced tenant-friendly laws firsthand, and tenants that knew how to exploit them. I don't want anyone to go through that. I have experienced markets where it can literally take a year to evict a tenant if they know how to play the game. Before you choose a market, do your homework.

Finding A Tenant

Filling vacant units is just a normal part of managing a multi-family investment. Do not shortcut the application and screening process. There are a lot of "professional renters" out there that take advantage of inexperienced landlords. They will put on this great front of being the perfect tenant during the lease screening process and turn out to be a "tenant from hell."

Every prospective tenant needs to fill out a comprehensive lease application. Make sure to obtain a credit report and a criminal history on every applicant. The effort must be made to verify employment. Someone should call previous landlords to see why they left and to ask if they would ever rent to them again.

Shelling out a little bit of money to check them out can help you from getting shell shock after they trash your unit and stick you with months of unpaid rent.

In my days of renting single-family homes and plexes, I would sometimes take tenants with less than perfect credit or other negative factors. I would require they pay very large deposits, as much as allowable by law. This would help protect me, if I need to evict them down the road.

I once leased this large five bedroom house in Denver to a gentleman with bad credit. I allowed him to move in with a huge deposit. Imagine my surprise one morning, when I'm reading the paper and there is a picture of that house. The article headline read, *"Making Money The Old-Fashioned Way."* The gentleman I rented to turned had a prostitute working in each bedroom. Of course, I evicted the tenant and was protected because of the large deposit.

Sample Rental Application

Have each adult applicant (18 or older) fill out a separate application.

Applicant Information

- Name (First, Middle, Last)
- Birth Date
- Social Security #
- Email Address
- Home Phone
- Cell Phone
- Driver's License #
- All Other Occupants' (Under 18) Birth Dates & Relationship

Rental History

- Current Residence
- Address, City, State, Zip
- Monthly Rent
- Date of Residence (From/To)
- Reason for Moving
- Was the rent paid before you moved?
- Were you asked to move?

168

- Owner/Manager's Name
- Phone Number

Previous Residence

- Address, City, State, Zip
- Monthly Rent
- Date of Residence(From/To)
- Reason for Moving
- Was the rent paid before you moved?
- Were you asked to move?
- Owner/Manager's Name
- Phone Number

Employment History

- Current Employer
  - Occupation
  - Employer Address
  - Employer's Phone
  - Dates of Employment
  - Name of Supervisor
  - Monthly Pay
- Previous Employer
  - Occupation
  - Employer Address
  - Employer's Phone
  - Dates of Employment
  - Name of Supervisor
  - Monthly Pay

Vehicles

- Include vehicles belonging to other proposed occupants.
- Make, Model, Color, Year, License Plate

Credit History

- Bank/Institution and Balance on Deposit or Balance Owed for the following accounts:
- Checking Account
- Savings Account
- Credit Card
- Auto Loan
- Additional Debt

References

- Name
- Phone Number
- Relationship

General Information

- Have you ever been late or delinquent on rent? Y/N
- Have you ever been party to a lawsuit? Y/N
- Have you ever been convicted of a felony? Y/N
- Have you ever filed for bankruptcy? Y/N
- Do you smoke? Y/N
- Do you have any pets? Y/N
- If yes, list type, breed, weight, and age.
- If yes to any of the above, please explain why.
- Why are you moving from your current address?
- We will be running a credit and background check. Is there anything negative in your credit or background check that you may want to address here?
- When can you move here?

Agreement & Authorization

I believe the statements I have made are true and correct. I hereby authorize a credit and/or criminal check to be made, verification of information I provided, and communication with any and all names listed on this application. I understand that any discrepancy or lack of information may result in the rejection of this application. I understand that this is an application to lease a residence and does not constitute a rental or lease agreement in whole or part. I further understand that there is a non-refundable fee to cover the cost of processing my application, and I will not receive a refund, even if I don't get the residence. Any questions regarding rejected applications must be submitted in writing and accompanied by a self-addressed, stamped envelope.

- Signature of Applicant
- Date
- Application Fee
- Date Paid in Full

Repairs & Maintenance

I believe in taking care of my residents. If they have a legitimate maintenance concern, I want to get it fixed as quickly as possible. Once the repair is completed,

I will then follow up to make sure it has been repaired to their satisfaction. That small action goes a long way toward keeping your tenants happy.

It is much better to keep tenants happy and in your properties as long as possible than to have frequent tenant turnover. When a tenant knows their concerns are heard, addressed and remedied, they will think twice about moving. Every time a unit turns over, you lose money. In addition, that unit will probably require repairs or upgrades that would not have been necessary if the tenant had stayed.

Even if you have a management company, keep a sharp eye on the maintenance of your units. Make repairs and maintenance items your priority. Choose a competent maintenance man who has the skills, experience, licensing, and insurance to protect your investments. Some well-timed, proactive, preventative maintenance work can go a long way to saving you from having to replace an expensive item, such as A/C condensers, furnaces, appliances, or the roof.

Your policies regarding rent and other building rules should be clearly explained verbally to each tenant.

Rent Collection

I am very firm on rent collection. I have found after decades of managing my own properties, if you allow someone to get behind in their rent, they will rarely, if ever, catch up. If a resident has not paid by the 5th of the month, they get a late notice. If they haven't paid by the 15th, I start the eviction process.

It is very important that you, or your property manager, clearly outline your rent collection policies verbally with every new tenant. This policy should be written down before you lease out your first unit. Don't just include the policy in the lease agreement. Your policies regarding rent and other building rules should be clearly explained verbally to each tenant. Actually taking the time to explain your rent collection and other property policies to the tenant at lease signing has a significant impact on reducing problems. Of course, you or your team will state the rules and regulations with a smile and a friendly tone, but they should know exactly where you, and they, stand before they get the key.

When it comes time to evict a tenant (notice I said "when" not "if"), remember that every state has different eviction laws. If you take matters in your own hands and do not go through the legal eviction process, you could very easily end up in court and your deadbeat tenant could win the case.

That means that evicting a tenant is not shutting off the electric or water. It is not changing the locks while they are at work. It is not showing up one day and forcibly moving their personal stuff to the curb. If you try any of these tricks, you will deeply regret it.

When you set up your rent collection policy, make sure you know the state's laws on the eviction process and find a good local eviction attorney. The laws will stipulate every step in the process, including the amount of time between notices.

If you happen to be in a state with an extremely long or expensive eviction process or you are dealing with a "professional tenant," you could try exchanging "cash for keys." The idea is you pay them to leave. Let's say the tenant owes you one month's rent, and an eviction process takes a minimum of 30 days. You are now looking at 60 days of lost income, plus the turn-around time to fix and re-rent the unit. Why not kindly and calmly approach the tenant and offer to waive the back rent, and possibly even give them a little money, if they move out within 7 days. Sometimes you are much better to cut your losses.

Choosing A Property Management Company

When attempting to locate the right property manager, I recommend only considering property management companies that have an office in the general area of your property. Before you choose the closest PM, ask if they own or have an ownership interest in any properties that are near yours. If they do, that would create a conflict of interest.

Look for a company that is managing or has experience in managing properties that are similar in size and type to your property. I would look for mid-sized property management companies and avoid very small ones. I would also avoid those gigantic firms where you are just an account number.

If you will be evaluating a management company, it can be a great idea to mystery shop. Come in as if you are looking for an apartment to rent and go through the preliminary process of renting. This is a great way to gauge their professionalism and people skills.

What To Expect

The duties of a property management company generally include the following areas:

- Determining Market Rent
- Rent Adjustments
- Rent Collections
- Locating and Screening Tenants
- Writing Leases
- Evictions and Move-Outs
- Maintenance and Repairs
- Payment of Expenses
- Financial Reports and Summaries

By the time you are ready to bring on a property manager, you are going to want to back off from the day-to-day operations. It is important when establishing the relationship with the management company that, they understand they will be dealing with the nitty-gritty stuff, but that you will be the ultimate decision maker. You will want to set a maximum threshold on expenses within the written agreement. If a specific expense or incident crosses a certain point, they will be required to obtain your approval.

If you have decided to have your investment managed from the very start, you can utilize their experience during the due diligence process. They can help you to evaluate a property to purchase. They can bring their employees to help with the physical inspection, building condition, records and lease inspections. Not only will this better help you and them to understand the property, but it will also save you considerable time and money.

The Interview

At this point in the evaluation, do not think about their fee. Focus on their service package; how they handle themselves; their confidence level; their level of communication skills, and their knowledge of the market area. Here are some questions to discuss during the interview process:

Renting the Property

- What is your procedure?
- What mediums do you use to advertise a rental?
- What is your average "make ready" turnaround time?
- Screening Tenants
- Do you personally interview the applicant?
- What company do you use to perform a credit report?
- What other screening steps do they use?
- Do they have a standard lease agreement? If so, get a copy.
- Who designed your lease agreement? Hopefully, an attorney.

- When was it last updated?
- Do they explain the lease and their procedures verbally to the tenant at lease up?
- How do you determine what is the fair market rent for a unit?
- How do you determine when to increase the rent?

Maintenance and Repairs

- How do they deal with these issues?
- When do you contact the owner for authorization?
- Who does the repairs?
- Are they licensed?
- Are they employed by your company or are they a sub-contractor?
- What is their hourly rate for each type of work?
- Do you conduct periodic inspections? When?
- How do you handle an emergency repair?

Rent Collections and Delinquencies

- What procedures do they follow to make sure you receive your monthly rental payments?
- What do they do if the tenants are late?
- How long do they wait until filing for eviction?

Reporting

- How regularly do you report on rental collections?
- Should I expect monthly or quarterly statements?
- What management software do you use?

Communication

- How often do you contact your property owners?
- What method do you use to contact them? Email, text, or phone calls?

Contract

- May I take a sample copy of your contract to review?
- What is your termination policy in case there are problems?

Licensing and Insurance

- Are you licensed?
- What organizations do you belong to?
- Do you carry liability insurance? If so, what are the limits?
- Do you carry Errors and Omissions Insurance (E&O)? If so, what are the limits on that policy?

Testimonials

- Request the names and phone numbers of three to five clients with at least one of them being a past client. Give them a call, and see what they have to say about the company.

The Service Fee

Property management companies will charge between 3 to 8% of the gross rent with the average being between 3 to 6%. In addition to this flat percentage rate, you will regularly have to pay a leasing fee when an empty unit gets leased. This fee covers the additional advertising and screening. You could expect to pay ½ to a full month's rent for a leasing fee.

A new practice getting attention is an a la carte type of service. You can pick and choose what services they provide. The fee can be negotiated, either monthly or based on a specific event.

Some property investors want to manage the repairs and rent collection, but they are more than willing to pay a leasing fee to a PM in order to get a qualified tenant. Others will qualify the tenant but hire a PM to manage the collections, bill payments and maintenance. It all depends on what services you want them to provide.

The Contract

You will want to examine the contract very carefully. Buried in these contracts can be allowances for all sorts of charge backs. I have heard of so many property owners that were shocked when, in addition to their percentage of the gross income, they were also charged for management software, cell phones, office supplies, and a ton of other nickel-and-dime charges that can quickly add up. Look over the contract with a fine tooth comb, or better yet, have your attorney analyze it.

Many property management companies also broker properties on the side. I would never give a property management company an exclusive right to sell or purchase your property. The agreement should also have an immediate right to cancel. Most PM companies want 30 days' notice. It puts you in a dangerous position when a property management company no longer has a requirement to protect your interests.

Reports

The monthly reports you receive from your property manager should include:

- Income and expense statement
- List of all payments made
- Current rent roll
- List of all vacancies
- List of all delinquencies
- Annual budget
- A monthly narrative of what is happening with the property's operations

Added Services

It is a great idea to ask your property manager to do a quarterly market survey of your competitors. That survey will show what your competitors are charging for their rental units. It will help you compare your rent and amenities to your competition. Plus, it is a sly way to remind your PM to keep on top of the market rents for lease renewals and new tenant leases.

Chapter 20
Adding Value To Your Property

Multifamily properties are my favorite asset class because of the incredible ability to pro-actively impact the value by improving the net operating income (NOI. There are few other investments that have such freedom to adjust the market value of a property through a few simple management decisions.

Increase Value Through Rent Increases

Even small rent increases will go directly to the bottom line and create a massive impact on your market value. For example a $20 monthly rent increase on a 100 unit building will create a $24,000 annual increase in the NOI. If you have a cap rate of 6%, you have just increased the value of your investment by $400,000 ($24,000 ÷.06).

Increase Value Through Expense Adjustments

Remember that your net operating income is directly connected to the market value of your investment. You can have the same impact on your net operating income if you reduce the expenses, and even more if you also increase the rent. You can either work to reduce the operating expenses or pass through some expenses to the tenants.

One way to pass through expenses, would be to institute a RUBS (Ratio Utility Billing System) where the utilities are billed back to the residents. Let's say that you have a 24-unit apartment building that is serviced by a large HVAC system. This means that the heating and air would normally be included in the rent. That can really add up. Well, that is where RUBS comes in.

This method uses the "Designated Occupant Factor." The idea behind this is that an apartment with one resident will use less utility usage than an apartment with four occupants. This method of bill allocation factors in the number of occupants per unit and divides the bill accordingly. How is it calculated?

First, you would determine the number of occupants in each unit. You then take that month's utility bill, of say $1,200, and subtract the percentage of common area. If you have an 11,300 square foot building with 500 square feet of common area, 4.4% of the bill would be removed (500 sf. of common area ÷ 11,300 gross building area = .044). The remaining portion is allocated to the tenants based on occupancy.

From here a designated occupant factor is determined. Here is an example of the standard division:

1 Person =	1.0	(1 Person pays 100% of 1)
2 People =	1.6	(2 People pay 60% more than 1)
3 People =	1.9	(3 People pay 30% more than 2)
4 People =	2.2	(4 People pay 30% more than 3)
5 People =	2.5	(5 People pay 30% more than 4)
6 People =	2.8	(6 People pay 30% more than 5)

Now in our example, we have a 24-unit building which is occupied as this chart indicates:

Unit	Occupants	Factor	Unit	Occupants	Factor
1	1	1.0	13	2	1.6
2	3	1.9	14	2	1.6
3	2	1.6	15	1	1.0
4	4	2.2	16	3	1.9
5	1	1.0	17	2	1.6
6	1	1.0	18	2	1.6
7	2	1.6	19	4	2.2
8	5	2.5	20	1	1.0
9	2	1.6	21	2	1.6
10	4	2.2	22	1	1.0
11	1	1.0	23	1	1.0
12	1	1.0	24	4	2.2
Total Factor		**36.9**			

Based on the above information, this is how it gets broken down:

Property Utility Bill	$1,500	
Rentable Area	x .956	Common Area = 4.4%
Total Amount to Allocate	**$1,434**	
Total Occupancy Factor	36.9	
1 Person Occupancy Rate	**$38.86**	**($1,434 ÷ 36.9)**

Now that we have the cost for a single occupancy, we apply the factor to each unit.

Unit	Factor	Utility Bill	Unit	Factor	Utility Bill
1	1.0	$ 38.86	13	1.6	$ 62.18
2	1.9	$ 73.83	14	1.6	$ 62.18
3	1.6	$ 62.18	15	1.0	$ 38.86
4	2.2	$ 85.49	16	1.9	$ 73.83
5	1.0	$ 38.86	17	1.6	$ 62.18
6	1.0	$ 38.86	18	1.6	$ 62.18
7	1.6	$ 62.18	19	2.2	$ 85.49
8	2.5	$ 97.15	20	1.0	$ 38.86
9	1.6	$ 62.18	21	1.6	$ 62.18
10	2.2	$ 85.49	22	1.0	$ 38.86
11	1.0	$ 38.86	23	1.0	$ 38.86
12	1.0	$ 38.86	24	2.2	$ 85.49
	Grand Total	**$1,433.93**			

As you can see from the calculation, all but the common area has been proportionately allocated to all the units based on the number of occupants. This would be billed monthly after receiving the utility bill. The landlord is still responsible for paying the utilities for the common area.

Charging back utilities to the tenants can encourage the tenants to take responsibility for their utility usage. They will not waste as much water or wear a sweater while the air is on because now they are paying for it. This method also creates fewer problems with tenants than a simple equal division of the bill across the total number of units. You will need to be prepared, however, to answer quite a few questions at the start. By walking them through the calculations, they will understand this is a fair allocation of the expenses. You may want to even include a copy of the original bill as proof.

This can be a very powerful way to quickly improve your NOI, and thereby, increase your property value. It should be noted, however, that this will typically impact your vacancies in some fashion, at least initially. Before you implement this policy, check to see if your competitors are also using RUBS. If not, then you could very easily lose residents, especially if you are also charging market rents.

I know these calculations are a bit complex. There are companies you can hire that provide RUBS as a service to your building. They handle everything including billing.

Some RUBS companies include:

- Multifamily Utility Company http://www.multifamilyutility.com/rubs.html
- American Conservation and Billing Solutions http://www.amcobi.com/index.php/utility-billing-services/ratio-utility-billing-services-rubs

Check with your property manager to see if they are familiar with and utilize this process.

Increase Liquid Assets Through Refinancing

I prefer to think of myself as a real estate "buyer" not a "seller." My strategy when buying property is to hold it forever. Sometimes I may require a "liquidity event" to give my investors a return of capital, or I may need to liquidate capital to acquire another property. My favorite method to create liquid equity is through refinancing.

If you have purchased a property for a good price and then repositioned it through income increases, expense reductions or utility pass-through, you should have been able to greatly increase the value of your asset. In this example, notice how these few changes have dramatically affected the market value:

Subject Property	24 Unit Apartment	
Purchase Price	$1,200,000	$50,000/Unit
Net Operating Income	**$93,600**	
Monthly Rent Increase	$20 per Unit	($20 x 24 Units) x 12 Mo = $5,760
Increased Gross Income	$5,760	($93,600 + $5,760)
Expense Reduction	$17,208	(RUBS: $1,434/mo. x 12 months)
Total Income Increase	$22,968	
Adjusted NOI	$116,568	
Capitalization Rate	8%	
Current Market Value	**$1,457,000**	($116,568 NOI ÷ .08 Cap Rate)

Chapter 21
Success Vs Fulfillment

My greatest mentor, Tony Robbins, is always talking about the difference between the science of achievement and the art of fulfillment. He has identified that there is a science to achievement and success, but the act of feeling fulfilled in life is an art. There is nothing worse than being a financial success and not being happy. It is fulfillment that gives you that happiness.

What creates that feeling of fullness in your life? That feeling of utter contentment and satisfaction is different for everyone. What makes you feel fulfilled is not what makes me feel fulfilled. While the source of the fulfillment differs from person to person, there is one universal means to fulfillment. I will talk about it in just a minute.

I've had a lot of ups and downs in my life – just like everyone else, I suppose. I am not telling you this next story to brag, but more to exemplify this point. My goal here is to inspire you to add this richness and fulfillment into your life.

At one point about 10 years ago, I thought I had reached the pinnacle of success. As I mentioned earlier, I dreamed of owning a big house on the beach, and I had built this incredible $8 million dollar, 10,000 square-foot mansion on a beautiful beach in Sarasota. It was actually a "gulf to bay" home, because I owned the beach on one side and the bay in back, which had its own boathouse.

Here I am floating in this amazing pool with two beautiful waterfalls pouring into it, looking up at my gigantic home that contained every luxury I could imagine. It was a pure testament to my ego. It was then that I realized even though I had all this "success," I was depressed. I was shocked and wondered, "How can I have all of this and still be depressed?" I felt hollow inside. Something was lacking, yet I had – or thought I had – everything that I could ever want.

When I look back now, I realize there were two things going on. One, I had achieved this massive goal that led me to think, "Is this all there is in life?" I needed a vision for the future. I needed to have another long-term goal. As the Good Book says, *"Without a vision, the people perish."* This reminds me to

It is fulfillment that gives you happiness.

emphasize the importance of always having other goals outlined before you achieve your current goals. But I digress; this is not the point of this story. The second element that I neglected to take into consideration was the need to feel fulfilled and what it really takes to create that. As I said earlier, "Success is a science, but feeling fulfilled is an art."

Let me share with you what will always make you feel fulfilled. Oh sure, I felt a measure of fulfillment when I bought the Lamborghini. I swelled with pride as we moved into our *You need to help others.* beach-side castle. But it was a fleeting feeling. It didn't last. It felt more hollow and empty over time. If you want to feel a deep sense of fulfillment, one that is solid and lasts, then you need to contribute to something or someone beyond yourself. You need to help others.

Everything in this universe has something to contribute to the greater whole. If it does not contribute in some fashion, it is eliminated. The cycle of life is interdependent to all elements on this planet. We are all interconnected. For humans, contribution is actually a basic need. It is not a bonus factor or an add-on value. It is a basic human need. Unfortunately, it is a pretty underutilized need.

Giving Back

I want to tell you my story about giving back and what it has meant to me. Around the year 2000, I attended a Tony Robbins event and was incredibly inspired by the fact that he has fed millions of people through his annual Thanksgiving basket brigade.

With the help of my brother, I decided to feed five families in the Denver area that year. We got a list of five families from a local church and spent all afternoon buying groceries, turkeys and filling up boxes with food. The life-changing event happened at the third house.

I went by myself to deliver our gift to this family. When I got to the door and the woman who lived there came of out the house and saw the food, she just started crying. Then her five children came out and they all started crying. By this time, I was crying, too. I was hooked. I finally felt like I meant something, that I was doing something that was worthwhile. I got a taste of that feeling of fulfillment.

The next year, I fed 50 families. The year after that, I fed 100. The year after that, 200, then 400, then 800 and then in 2006, I was privileged to help 1,600 families. I got so much pleasure and fulfillment out of doing that, and I had paid for it all myself. You all know about the crash that happened in 2007 and 2008. About that time, I formed the Tiny Hands Foundation (TinyHandsFoundation.org) and started accepting donations so I could keep helping more and more families. I pay all the operational expenses for the foundation, so every dime we receive goes to help the children. As of the printing of this book, we have fed over 65,000 children with full Thanksgiving or Christmas dinners.

This work has been my greatest joy and gives me the fulfillment that I have been talking about.

A few years ago we also started what we call the Backpack Brigade. We have given thousands of backpacks filled with school supplies to at-risk children in my area. We have also given thousands of teddy bears to local police departments for their officers to keep in their cars. When they encounter a child that has experienced a traumatic event, these bears help to comfort the child and bridge the gap between the child and the police officer. This work has been my greatest joy and gives me the fulfillment that I have been talking about.

In addition to my philanthropy work, I have also found that my podcast, "Lifetime Cash Flow through Real Estate Investing," is another way I'm giving back. Similar to my foundation, it is giving me incredible joy.

Anything that you can do to give back to anyone is a blessing and will give you that long-term feeling of fulfillment. If you can't do it financially, there are lots of things you can do that don't cost a dime.

- Help an elderly person.
- Ask the clerk in the store how they are doing.
- Compliment the person serving you.
- Decide to smile at everyone you walk by today.
- Give the gift of that smile or a kind word.

It is said: *when you give, it comes back to you tenfold.* I am here to tell you that it is the absolute truth. Life is not just about financial success. It is about being happy and fulfilled. While I love real estate, and am really good at it, I have found that giving back is what I needed to feel like my life meant something.

Rod Khleif with Sarasota Chief of Police Bernadette DiPino, at Teddy Bear Brigade: Provides thousands of teddy bears for community police department patrol cars to be given out by police officers to comfort children in distress.

Rod & His wife Tiffany at Back-to-School Backpack Brigade: Provides thousands of new backpacks filled with school supplies to community school children in need.

Rod & his wife Tiffany at Holiday Basket Brigade: Provides holiday gift baskets filled with food and Christmas toys to over 1,500 community children and families in need per year.

Chapter 22
Summary And Taking Action

Thank you for graciously allowing me to tell you a bit of my story. You've learned about the power of goal setting and finding your why. I have shared how I've used it to visualize and manifest many things in my life. You can do the same. You've learned that the most important thing to focus on when buying real estate is cash flow. The value of real estate is secondary to its ability to cash flow.

You have learned how to identify and evaluate a good market to buy in, the types and classifications of properties, how to find and negotiate properties, how to finance them, how to syndicate, the people you need on your team, how to be creative when you buy, how to do comprehensive due diligence on a property, and how to ultimately manage your asset.

You now have the basic framework to go out and immerse yourself in this exciting business. If you want to continue your education, please take a look at www.Rod Khleif.com.

There are tons of valuable free resources and content there for you. If you want to go deeper and really shorten your learning curve, I have an incredible course and coaching program. I recommend you continue your education, whether or not you use me or another resource, while you're also simultaneously out there looking at and evaluating deals. You want to be as competent as possible in this business, which will develop your confidence to give you the ability to influence. You also want to greatly enhance your intuition because it is an invaluable resource when you are evaluating deals.

Intuition comes from study and time, while you are enjoying learning this business. Be sure to associate pleasure with your learning process, because when you enjoy what you do, work is play. I equate learning this business and looking at prospective deals with hunting for treasure, and so should you.

Chapter 23
Now It's Your Turn

It's time to take action on your dreams. Push forward through the fear, and get outside your comfort zone. It's time to create the life you were meant to live.

It's important to take action immediately and start your journey. In the free companion course to this book that you can access at www.LifetimeCashFlowBook.com, I have a goal setting workshop you can watch. It includes a PDF worksheet you can print to work from.

The first step in your journey needs to be figuring out exactly what it is you want. The best way to do that is to spend the time to write out your goals and carefully document why each one is a must.

This revised edition of my book has a 90 day action plan so that you can take massive action towards owning multifamily properties and creating lifetime cash flow for yourself and your family. Now go take action my friend.

90 Day Action Plan

"Your life is either an example....or a warning."

Tony Robbins

"Growth requires you to temporarily surrender security and comfort."

John Maxwell

"You are far too smart to be the only thing standing in your way."

Jennifer Freeman

Week #1

Task #1: Set Short Term Goals

Set your real estate goals, and your life goals as well. And be sure to write why they are an absolute must for you to achieve. Make sure they're clear, measurable, and you have pictures of them posted where you see them often.

Task #2: Perform Self Evaluation

- What real estate experience do you have, even if it's buying your primary residence?
- What is your current financial status?
- Current employment status?
- How many hours do you work a week?
- How much time can you dedicate to investing each week?
- What is your Risk Tolerance?
- Are you Conservative or Aggressive?
- You can't have an Employee Mindset
- Must have a Business Mindset
- Remember Multifamily is less subjective....
- It is more empirical
- Your Investor Identity will change as you mature in this business.
- You may start smaller and then move into larger properties.
- How is your credit?
- What is your net worth
- Investment capital
- Possible potential investors
- Family/friends
- Mentor or Coach that can help guide you

Task #3: Select Your Target Market

You can start in your own backyard, but if too expensive, you can also research a place you've spent some time, a place where you know people, or a place you'd like to retire or enjoy going. You're looking for an emerging market with increasing historical income, jobs and population. Choose one of these and become an expert on it.

Task #4: Establish Your Investment Criteria

What size, class, type, units and areas are you interested in? Write it down.

Things Includes:

- Size
- Location (area)
- Class
- Type of Area
- Stabilized or Value Add
- Price Range

You Need Clearly Defined Investment Criteria For:

- Credibility with Brokers
- Credibility with Sellers
- Credibility with Investors
- Staying on Track
- Becoming an Expert in a Market

Other Things To Take Into Consideration When Establishing Criteria:

- Your Initial investment
- How you will handle Property Management
- What Loans are available for the property size you're considering
- Your Target area… how far is it from where you live?
- How much time do you have to devote to this exciting business?
- Your resources including friends, family and associates?

Task #5: Name Your Business

You need to form a business for credibility. Here are some tips to get you going:

- **Select a name that is easy to remember.** Most investors put words like; equity, capital, real estate, partners, investments,ventures, etc. behind another name.
- **Thoroughly check the name online.** Do a web search and see if anyone else is using the name. That does not necessarily mean you can't use it, but important information to know.
- **Go to your state's Secretary of State website** and do a name search to make sure your desired name is available.
- **Perform a trademark search** of your name. There are free sites that allow you to do trademark searches or you can do them directly on the government's site. www.USPTO.gov/Trademark
- Here are some resources for finding name options.
    - VisualThesaurus.com
    - Shopify
    - Business Name Generator,
    - NameMesh.com
    - Naminum.com
- **Check all social media platforms** like Facebook, Instagram, YouTube, Twitter and Linkedin to make sure nobody is using the name and lock the name up as quickly as you can on the platforms you intend to utilize.

Task #6: Check Domain Name on GoDaddy or Instant Domain Search

https://www.godaddy.com/

Go to GoDaddy.com and make sure your name or a rendition of your name is available to buy as a .com URL. Don't buy any of the other offered URL extensions like .biz etc. as they are not as powerful for you.

ACTION PLAN

https://instantdomainsearch.com/

This site will help you get the best domain for what you are looking for. It will show you options for all the extension, ideas for combinations of words if you can't find your exact domain, etc.

Task #7: Start Process to set up LLC for your Branding Company

You can use the company you form this week as the initial purchaser on your contracts. It's not as intimidating as it sounds. It's just a phone call.

It requires you to identify the owner, and I recommend more than one person. You can bring in your spouse or child to make it a multi-member LLC. You'll also need an address.

If you want to use a paid service, you can take a look at: http://bit.ly/2uGUWGo

If you want to DIY: Here is a great article to get you started, but if you are unclear, always consult an attorney before proceeding. http://bit.ly/2UgGgMX

Be sure to visit your social media platform of choice to claim your business name.

Week #2

Task #1: LoopNet Research for Brokers (Create List of Top 100 Brokers in Your Market)

Find brokers who are heavily marketing the size and type of properties that fit your criteria. Develop a relationship with them. Remember to follow up with them, and respect their time.

Look in Multifamily for Sale:

- Find a broker who has several of the type and size properties you're interested in for sale
- Tell them you're calling in regards to one of their LoopNet listings'.

Here is a sample script:

Hello, my name is_____, I'm an investor out of "your city", how are you today?

……I'm calling in regards to one of your LoopNet listings. It's "Shady Oaks"… is that property still available?……

……Great, I definitely want to see some more information on that. Before you send that, I do have a few quick questions.

What's the story on this property? Why is it for sale?…….

……Interesting… this sounds like it has potential. Here's my contact info:…..

Also, do you typically list properties similar to this one?

.........My partners and my criteria is"_____", and we're currently looking to acquire several properties within the next year. Feel free to send anything similar, I'll be sure to get back to you as soon as possible.

Valuing Brokers – Following Up

- Most people never follow up!
- Tell the broker why the deal didn't work for you with specifics from your analysis.
- The more detailed your response, the better.
- Refresh their memory on your exact investment criteria
- Always respect the broker's time.
- Look for ways to set yourself apart.

Task #2 Contact 3-5 New Brokers Every Week and Analyze Deals

With your list in hand and the script I laid out above, make sure to contact 3-5 new brokers every week. Set a specific day each week for this task to help you remember.

As you make each contact, drop that broker into your CRM (see task #7) so that you can keep tabs on who you've contacted and when. Schedule out a regular contact plan for each broker.

The goal isn't just to find a deal, but to keep yourself top-of-mind so that brokers will begin sending pocket listings to you. This process is always about developing long-term relationships with brokers, instead of a specific deal.

Task # 3: Contact 3-5 Property Management Companies over the Next Three weeks and Ask for Referrals to Other Team Members

If you're in real estate, you're in the people business. And the more people you can bring into your professional circle, the more deal flow you can expect.

In the same way you established relationships with brokers in task #2, reach out to property managers in your target market. Ask them about the market and learn as much as you can. Be sure to ask for connections to other professionals (brokers, lawyers, lenders, contractors) who you can utilize as well.

Task #4: Order Business Cards

Business cards can be very inexpensive. You can visit VistaPrint.com and print 500 cards for usually under $10 (check their website for their latest specials). You need legitimacy and to have something to hand out to Brokers, property managers, potential investors etc.

Task #5: Create 1-2 Page Preliminary Website for Your Investing Business

You can use these resources to help you:

- www.Oncarrot.com
- www.Leadpropeller.com
- www.Realeflow.com
- www.Fiver.com

Make sure to include your picture, what you do, and your investment criteria.

Task #6: Reach out to Three Potential Sponsors for Your Deals

As you get your feet wet in the market, you're going to come across deals that excite you. Take that energy and share it with at least 3 senior investors who might consider sponsoring you on a deal. You are just building relationships at this point but when you have an actual deal, be sure you present a full analysis and your business plan for that asset.

Task #7 Set up CRM or Excel Spreadsheet to Track Your Contacts

When you start contacting brokers, team members, sponsors, etc., it's easy to lose track of your communications. That's why you need a system for keeping track of your contacts.

In your CRM or spreadsheet, upload the names and contact information for all the people you contact as you push forward. Use tags and/or sort them into groups for easier searching.

Week #3

Task #1: Research And Find Your Local REI Meeting

As you know, this business is a team sport and networking is vital to an investor's success. Find your local real estate investment clubs (REIA) for both single family and multifamily investors. Attend meetings to connect with friends, peers and mentors.

You've got to find people who are doing what you're doing. You must be immersed in this business so you build your confidence as quickly as possible. You'll get synergy by being around people who are doing what you're doing.

National REIA Listing: https://nationalreia.org/find-a-reia/

Task #2: Research and Find Your Local Meetup Groups

REIA isn't the only place you can go to network with other investors. Meetup.com is a great resource for making new contacts. To expand your network of potential private money lenders, don't just focus on the real estate specific groups. Instead, broaden your scope to include more general finance/investing groups as well as topics that personally interest you.

If you can find them, groups with high net-worth individuals will be a great source of prospective investors. New relationships bring new opportunities to share what you're doing and invite other people to get involved.

Task #3: Get a Paper and Look In Classifieds

Not everybody is on the Internet these days, especially elderly apartment building owners. These folks will list their properties for sale in the only medium they're familiar with—the newspaper.

So, don't neglect your local daily news. Grab a copy, or look online in their real estate section, and you just might be surprised to find a deal where nobody else bothered to look.

Task #4: Contact Two Commercial Mortgage Brokers Each During the Next Three Weeks

Like you did with brokers last week, it's time to start building out your network of commercial lenders. From the referrals you asked for from brokers and property managers, start establishing relationships and describing your criteria, and start becoming more familiar with the financing process.

Task #5: Make a List of Family and Friends Who Might Be Interested in Investing

You're surrounded by more potential funders than you think. Friends and family members can serve as excellent investors your multifamily real estate business. If they've got an IRA or a 401(k), then there's no reason why you can't present them with an alternative investment vehicle.

Week #4

Task #1: Contact Five People in Your List of Family and Friends and Discuss Investing

The key to getting people on board isn't "selling" them, but letting them know what you're up to, and the kinds of opportunities you've seen out in the market. Reach out and influence your network with your excitement for multifamily real estate. When you do, don't forget to put these contacts into your CRM.

Task #2: Do Five Evaluations and Practice, Practice, Practice!

Successful investors seem to have an intuition about deals. The truth is, that deal-sense is a product of years of poring over and analyzing properties. There's no shortcut here. If you want to learn the art and science of spotting a deal, you need to get in there and practice by analyzing as many deals as possible.

Task #3: Register on Four Auction Sites

Deal flow is crucial in the multifamily business and auction sites are a great way to maintain your supply of potential acquisitions. Get onto popular sites like Hudson and Marshall, Williams and Williams, Xome, and RealtyBid. Set alerts to notify you when a new property hits within your target market.

Task #4: Contact 2-3 Local or Regional Banks And Ask About Loan Programs and Start Relationships

Last week, you started building relationships with commercial lenders. This week, add local banks to your list. These banks are easier to work with than the large national institutions. A solid relationship with your local or regional bank won't just bring you access to funds, it'll connect you with their REO department and another source of multifamily leads.

Week #5

Task #1: Check/Register on Other Brokerage Listing Sites

Don't content yourself with a just a few online sites. Remember, deal acquisition is a numbers game. The more places you look, the more leads you'll find. More leads leads to more practice analyzing deals and a higher likelihood that you'll find one worthy of an LOI.

Task #2: Contact Five More Potential Investors and Discuss What You're Doing

While you're building your deal flow, it's important that you continue to build your database of potential investors. This week, reach out to 5 more people on your list and talk about what you're seeing in the market. Bring the passion to these conversations so that you influence them positively.

Task #3: Prepare And Implement Craigslist Strategies

For Sale: Dedicate time to searching for deals on your local market's Craigslist page. Call owners that have listed multifamily properties for sale. Even if you're not sure about the deal, give them a call to practice those conversations and build your confidence.

For Rent: Don't just look at 'for sale' listings. Rental listings have one thing in common: vacancy. Look for units listed for rent by owner and give them a call. Try to find out what led to the vacancy and, more importantly, whether the owner is fed up enough with the property to discuss selling it.

Week #6

Task #1: If Your Target Market is Your Backyard, Drive Areas For a Full Day and Look for Run-Down Properties

Driving for dollars is a tried-and-true tactic for finding deals. So, mark out a day in your calendar and head out with your notepad and camera in hand. When you find a run-down multifamily, jot down the address and snap a few shots of the exterior. When you get home, look up the owner's contact info, drop them into your CRM, and reach out to see if they're interested in selling.

Task #2: Evaluate Five More Properties

Practice, practice, practice. Don't get lazy here. Repetition equals skill. Do a full evaluation, even if you're not sure if/how you can make the deal work. See what price the deal would make sense to you and your investors.

Task #3: Contact Five More Potential Investors and Build Relationships

Keep your head down and do the contact work. Again, you are just building friendships. Tell them what you're doing and show the passion. If you're passionate, you'll inspire and influence them. Keep building that investor database.

Task #4: Spend 15 Minutes Each Day Checking Craigslist and the Newspaper

Print isn't dead yet and can still be a potential source of deals, This week, block off time in your daily schedule to check these two underutilized sources for deals. You may be surprised at what you can find.

Task #5: Contact a Residential Broker and Start Relationship in Case They Come Across a Multifamily Property

While you should definitely focus your time and energy on commercial brokers, developing relationships with residential brokers in your target market is a must.

Residential brokers come across commercial listings from time to time and do not know how to handle them. Make sure you ask your residential broker to put an alert in their MLS system for any apartment deals that show up. That you're ready to buy.

Task #6: Start a Relationship With a Syndication Attorney

If syndication isn't on your radar yet, it should be. You may just be starting, but an important part of building a successful multifamily business is envisioning your success and preparing for it. There's going to come a time when you need to put a syndicate together in order to make a move on a larger property. Start that relationship.

Week #7

Task #1: Run Ads for Multifamily Properties on Craigslist

Last week, I had you start scouring Craigslist for opportunities. Now, it's time to create an ad to see what you can drum up. Keep in mind, you won't be the only one posting on Craigslist. So, focus on writing a tight, clean ad and reposting it frequently.

Task #2: Run Ads Looking for Partners on Craigslist

In addition to your ad for multifamily property, put out a call for partners. Start by focusing on their pain points—stock market uncertainty, low-yield savings rates, etc.—and then present real estate investment as a safe, attractive alternative.

Share results and invite readers to get involved with a clear, concise call to-action. Remember, you can't advertise a specific deal unless you're doing a 506(c) syndication to Accredited Investors only. You are just building relationships with prospects.

Task #3: Evaluate Five More Deals

Can you see a theme here? Don't stop evaluating deals. Work time into your schedule every day to scour your sources and run promising leads through a full analysis. Keep it up and you'll not only hone your analytic skills, but you'll be sure to uncover your next deal.

Task #4: Talk to Five More Potential Investors to Invest in Your Deals

Keep reaching out to potential equity partners. When you do, pay close attention to the particular stories and aspects of the business that resonate with the people you're talking to.

Distill your best material into a written script, internalize it, and use it as a guide in future conversations. You are building relationships for future investment in your deals.

Task #5: See if Code Violations or Evictions Might be an Opportunity for Deals

Check with your target market county or city for recent code violation lists and/or lists of evictions. Treat these properties like the ones you'd find when out driving for dollars. Drop them into a database and reach out to each owner individually. Focus on pain points: "are you tired of dealing withe victions."

Task #6 Reach Out to Four More Different Types of Lenders: Local, Bridge, Agency, and Hard Money

Sometimes, you're going to have to get creative in order to make a deal happen. In this business, the most successful investors are the ones who gather as many tools in their bag as possible so that they never find themselves without an option. Non- traditional lending sources are a crucial part of that toolkit. Keep building your database.

Week #8

Task #1: Enhance Your Business Website to Include the Members of Your Team You've Aligned With

Now that you've added some members to your team, including potential sponsors, update your website to reflect your thickened presence.

Always get permission to add someone to your website.

Potential funders and partners want to see you're not a lone ranger. Having other names and faces associated with you will add an important element of legitimacy to your business.

Task #2: Evaluate Five More Deals

As you get more and more comfortable with your target market, be sure to stand back and think about its overall shape. Where are you seeing the best deals? What is the path of progress? What areas would you not want to collect rent in at night? Which brokers specialize in which areas?

Task #3: Talk to Five More Potential Investors

By now, you should be getting comfortable with your pitch. You should also have a sizeable list of investors you've already reached out to in your CRM. Keep adding to it, but don't forget to communicate consistently with the people who are already on the list.

If you haven't already, look for subtle ways to stay top of mind with your previous contacts—a handwritten note, a short email, a phone call, or sending an article you curate speaking to the benefits of multifamily investing or touting your target market.

Task #4: Submit an LOI on a Property with LOI or Submit a Sales Contract

Over the past two months, you've been analyzing deals, talking to brokers, and getting your feet wet in the market. Submit an LOI based on your numbers and stand firm in the negotiation. If the deal doesn't fly, learn from your experience and move on to the next one. You haven't wasted your time.

Task #5: Start Your Own Multifamily Meetup Group

Meetup groups are a great place to meet like-minded individuals. They're also a great place to find partners and investors. Whether you've already joined a group or not, start your own multifamily group. Even if it only starts out with a couple of people, you are immersed in the business and talking shop. The more you talk about this business the more confident you will become.

Week #9

Task #1: Submit an LOI

Did last week's LOI get shot down? No sweat; write another one. It could take you as many as 20 LOIs to finally get a contract on a property. That's a normal part of the business, and it should encourage you to keep up with your deal flow and analysis. When a property makes sense, don't hesitate.

Write an LOI, then let your due diligence confirm your initial analysis.

Task #2: Negotiate Terms With Seller

If you submit an LOI or contract directly to a seller be sure to prepare by learning everything you can about the property and its owner. Decide beforehand which compromises and concessions you're going to make. Be prepared to give a little, but make sure you know exactly what you'll need to get in return.

Task #3: Start Looking for the Best Financing Options

By now, you've already built relationships with lenders of all different kinds. Now it's time to reach out to your contacts and look for the lender/product that's going to work best with this deal. Not every lender is created equal, so make sure to check in with several of them before you make a decision.

Task #4: Send Teaser to Potential Investors if Syndicating

If you plan to syndicate this property, then it's time to send out a concise teaser about the upcoming deal. Share the property details along with your summary analysis and your projections for the next several years. Give investors a preview of what you're offering and the terms your offering for their participation.

Week #10

Task #1: Come to Terms With Seller and Settle on Final LOI

If you haven't already, wrap-up negotiations with the seller and get an LOI accepted.

Task #2: Send LOI to Attorney and Have Him Prepare Purchase and Sale Agreement

An LOI is basically a glorified handshake agreement. It's not a contract. For that, you'll need to send your LOI to an attorney who can draw up the appropriate legal documents. Be sure to work closely with the attorney to ensure you give yourself plenty of time for due diligence as well as all the necessary contingencies in case you need to back out of the deal.

Task #3: Make Due Diligence/ Inspection Preparations

Once the seller signs the contract, your due diligence clock starts. As your lawyer draws up the paperwork, reach out to all the inspectors and contractors you need in order to check out the property. At the same time, start collecting all the paperwork you'll need to review as part of your due diligence (see checklist). Ideally do not have your due diligence clock start until you've received all of the seller's documents you requested.

Task #4: Get Syndication Paperwork Ready

You should have contacted your syndication attorney once you had an accepted LOI and started work with them on preparing all the necessary paperwork. Here's what you'll need:

A Private Placement Memorandum (PPM) –this document explains the risks of the investment and how the offering will be run, along with details about the property.

An LLC Operating or LP Partnership Agreement –this is the investment contract between you and your investors.

A Subscription Agreement –this is where investors certify that they meet the financial qualifications and understand the risks involved.

A Property Package –this document describes the property itself, what you plan to do with it, income/expense projections, and acquisition costs.

Week #11

Task #1: Do all of Your Due Diligence

Depending on your contract, you'll likely have approx. 30 days from the date of receiving the sellers documents to complete all of your due diligence. Now is the time to be methodical; follow your checklists down to the last detail. Don't miss anything here and don't let your excitement press you into cutting corners or turning a blind eye to red flags. Leave no stone unturned.

Task # 2: Prepare a Loan Package for Your Lender

Just like you, lenders have their own due diligence to conduct. To that end, you can expect a fat stack of paperwork to fill out and documentation to provide for your deal. As you work on your due diligence, be sure to stay on top of all of the lender's requests in a timely manner.

Task #3: Firm up Commitments for Equity From Investors/Partners

If you're syndicating, now is the time to start getting signatures on all of the required paperwork. If you're doing a private money deal, then work with your attorney to formalize the funding arrangements. If you're working with partners and/or a sponsor, check in with your lender for their specific requirements. When it comes to funding/financing, you can never be too proactive. If you let things slip, you'll find yourself without the funds you need to close.

Week #12

Task #1: Keep Going on Due Diligence to Prepare to Close in 30 Days. Look Under Every Rock.

If you haven't yet cleared your due diligence period, keep going. Leave no stone unturned as you get to know every detail about this property. In the event that you have to renegotiate for the deal to make sense, be sure you have backup for your argument. Do not re-negotiate unless something significant was discovered in your due diligence.

Task #2: Firm up Equity From Your Investors/Private Lenders

If you haven't finished firming up commitments from investors and partners, now is the time to get it done. You don't want one your investors backing out in the 11th hour and leaving you no time to find another source of funds. Expect 25% of your equity commitments to back out. That is why you always oversubscribe.

Task #3: Provide All Required Documentation to Your Lender

Throughout the underwriting process, your lender is going to ask you to jump through one hoop after the next. Take it all in stride and get your lender what they need as quickly as possible. If you're working with a strong lender, they'll get you over the finish line.

Task #4: Prepare to Close in 30-45 days!!

Once you've got your due diligence completed and your lending squared away, you're on a clear path towards closing. On your way there, work on solidifying contracts with your vendors (property management, landscaping, etc.)

Task #5: Set up a Management Company LLC

Your attorney will also usually set up an LLC for the management of your property which will have the general partners (or KP's) interests in it. It will outline the arrangement between the KP's. The management LLC will own the General Partner's membership interests in the property specific LLC.

Task #6: Set up Property LLC

Your attorney will set up a separate LLC for the ownership of the property outlining preferred return to equity investors if any, and the splits between the general partners (you and other Key Principles or KP's) and your passive equity investors.

Task #7 Open Partnership and Property Bank Accounts

To keep yourself protected, be sure to open separate bank accounts for the partnership and the property itself. Never commingle money between different entity accounts or with your personal finances.

Congratulations!

Whether you have closed your first deal or not, congratulations are in order - you now have the knowledge to take down any multifamily property. I encourage you to keep reviewing and referring to this task list. Being diligent will help you develop the necessary skills and **competence breeds confidence.**

So, Where Do You Go From Here?

Well, my podcast; "Lifetime CashFlow through Real Estate Investing" and my website www.Rod Khleif.com were created to help aspiring real estate investors like yourself. That's where I share real estate tips, interviews, inspirational videos, and much more. All of the information posted on the website and podcast is free, so I hope you check it out. I look forward to serving you there.

If you apply the guidelines in this book and work to build your confidence, knowledge, and experience, I am convinced that you can also make a success of multifamily real estate investments. If you remember anything from this book, remember the new rule of real estate investment: It is all about cash flow, cash flow, cash flow.

I salute you for getting through this book on your way to your own lifetime cash flow. If you'd like to let me know what you thought of this book, send me a quick message on Facebook at @RodKhleifOfficial.

Thanks Again!

Let's Connect!

If you'd like to connect with me personally on social media, follow:

Facebook: https://www.facebook.com/RodKhleifofficial

LinkedIn: https://www.linkedin.com/in/RodKhleif

Instagram: https://www.instagram.com/Rod_Khleif

Twitter: https://twitter.com/RodKhleif

Please feel free to send me a direct message on any social channel. I love getting them and I respond to each one.

You can ask me a question, or leave a comment.

Talk soon!

Want To Have Rod's Team Work With You To Create Your Own 90-Day Multifamily Action Plan?

If you have the desire to build Lifetime Cashflow for yourself and your family by joining a group of motivated, supportive, and successful apartment investors with over 45,000 units.

Scan the code using your smartphone camera to book your call with Rod's team to apply:

or go to https://calendly.com/rk-success-agents/lcfbook

Join hundreds of students in every corner of the United States and Canada, Mexico and Europe.

The Warrior Community is our group of motivated and engaged real estate investors, who are each taking massive action to build a portfolio of multifamily properties for legacy cash flow by implementing Rod's strategies for personal and financial success.

Think you might be a fit? Scan the code below using your smartphone camera to book a call with Rod's team to apply!

The FREE
Lifetime CashFlow Companion Course

www.LifetimeCashFlowBook.com

Congrats on reading the book all the way through. You have taken the first step in creating *lifetime cash flow*. If you have not done so already, go to LifetimeCashFlowBook.com

You will get exclusive access to the FREE Companion Course I created for you.

You will have access to:

- Hours of video training
- Valuable content that will help you get the most out of the book
- A *full list* of resources and links mentioned in the book

The materials in this FREE course are organized by the sections and chapters in the book, making it very easy to follow along. I have also included tons of bonuses, including interviews and bonus videos.

I will also be adding additional materials on an ongoing basis so go ahead and visit the website below for **Instant Access.**

See you on the inside!

www.LifetimeCashFlowBook.com

Go visit <ins>www.MultiFamilyCommunity.com</ins> right now

and join this incredible free peer group!

You are invited to join the Multifamily Community Facebook Group

Here is what you will find inside the private group:

- Peer-to-Peer mentoring;
- Networking with potential partners and investors;
- A passionate group of people all interested in multifamily investing;
- Industry experts AND...
- My team and I answering questions to accelerate your learning curve.

Fans and readers of *"How to Create Lifetime community CashFlow Through Multifamily Properties"* make up an incredible community of motivated action takers that want more our of life. As the writer of the Lifetime CashFlow book, it was my responsibility to create an online space where aspiring multifamily real estate investors could go to connect, share ideas, ask questions, get encouragement, peer mentor, find accountability partners, and learn and grow in this exciting business.

Just go to MultiFamilyCommunity.com to join the "Multifamily Real Estate Investing Community" on Facebook with over 40,000 members. Here you'll be able to connect with an incredible peer group of investors who are already taking action on their dreams of building *lifetime cash flow* with *multifamily properties.*

You will be blown away by the caliber of the members in this community. Go there to give, but expect to also get incredible value from this incredible group of investors.

I check up on the group regularly and moderate the community. I look forward to seeing you there!

The Lifetime Cashflow Through Real Estate Investing Podcast was #1 in the Business, Education and Real Estate Sections of iTunes for over two years and has been downloaded over 11 million times. The podcast grants you access to expert real estate investors, syndicators, lenders, property managers and advisors. These experts share their stories, tips and advice on how they successfully built their businesses, and their fortunes, through multifamily real estate investing.

Host Rod Khleif is a seasoned and passionate real estate investor who has personally owned and managed over 2,000 properties so far in his career. Rod has combined his passion for real estate investing with his personal philosophies of self-actualization, goal setting, envisioning, and manifesting success to become one of America's top real estate investment professionals.

If you're looking for financial freedom t hrough m ultifamily r eal estate investing and want to learn strategies from some of the best real estate investors in the country... then this is the podcast for you.

We are only interested in adding value to our listeners and helping them find financial success.

Acknowledgments

I am deeply grateful for the love of the most amazing woman on the planet. My incredibly sweet, loving and beautiful wife, Tiffany. With her unwavering love, support and wisdom, there is no goal that seems out of reach. Thank you, my love.

This book is dedicated to my two fathers; Baheej Khleif and Donald Jacobs. I lost them both in the last three years, which was much too soon. Baheej taught me about the importance of education, positive attitude and graciousness. Donald taught me about having an incredible work ethic, integrity and patience. He also taught me about the importance of family.

To my mom and my incredible brothers, Albert, Edgar and Kevin. I would not be here without your love, friendship and support all of these years.

To my two amazing and brilliant children, Alex and Myles. You are both the light of my life and God's greatest gift to me. I am very proud of each of you.

I need to thank my greatest mentor, Tony Robbins. Tony changed my life 16 years ago, and I have never looked back. I have been blessed to be able to experience Tony's wisdom and passion several times a year for the last 16 years. I continually learn from this incredible man.

Other incredible teachers in my life include J. Scott Scheel, Frank McKinney, Zig Ziglar, Jack Canfield, John Gray, Tom Hopkins, and Wayne Dyer.

I am blessed to have some of the most incredible friends in the world. My oldest and dearest friend, Peter Austin. Also, Kevin Bupp, Lori Taylor, Joe Shelton, Ralph Zuckerman, and Peter Turo. We can go months without talking but always pick up where we left off. I love and am grateful for,each of you.

Thank you to my amazing podcast listeners and course and coaching clients. You guys rock!

It's impossible to thank everyone that has impacted my life and helped me on this incredible journey. I apologize to all my friends, employees, fans and supporters that are not listed here. I am very grateful for you.

Contributors

Special thanks to Kim Lisa Taylor for rewriting the Entity and Syndication chapters of this book. I highly recommend Kim for anyone needing an SEC attorney for syndicating multifamily. Kim's contact information is Kim@SyndicationAttorneys.com.

Special thanks to Scott Maurer with Advanta IRA. Scott rewrote the IRA section of this book to be factually accurate. I personally use Scott and Advanta for my Roth IRA. Scott's contact information is SMaurer@ AdvantaIRAGroup.com

Special thanks to Mark Sullivan, Bethany Smith, and Michelle Morgan for their help with editing this book.

About The Author

Rod Khleif is an entrepreneur, real estate investor, multiple business owner, author, mentor and community philanthropist. He is passionate about business, life, success and giving back.

As one of the country's top real estate investors, Rod has personally owned and managed over 2,000 properties.

Rod is Host of the #1 Ranked iTunes Real Estate Podcast "The Lifetime Cash Flow Through Real Estate Investing Podcast" which has been downloaded over 11 million times. He is also the Founder of the Lifetime Cash Flow Academy.

As an accomplished entrepreneur, Rod has built several successful multi-million dollar businesses.

As a community philanthropist, Rod founded and directs The Tiny Hands Foundation, which has bene ited more than 100,000 community children and families in need.

Khleif has combined his passion for real estate investing and business development coaching with his personal philosophy of goal setting, envisioning and manifesting success to become one of America's top real estate investment and business development trainers.

Meet Rod and receive free training at <u>www.RodKhleif.com.</u>

Endnotes

1. Federal Housing Finance Agency (FHFA), HPI 4Q 2015 News Release (February 25, 2016), 16, http://www.fhfa.gov/
AboutUs/Reports/ReportDocuments/HPI4Q2015_2252016.pdf

2. Compounded annual appreciation only. No other value changes.

3. U.S. Department of Housing and Urban Development, Affordable Housing, http://portal.hud.gov/hudportal/
HUD?src=/program_offices/comm_planning/afforda blehousing/, (April 14, 2016).